The Mother of Invention

ALSO BY NEALE DONALD WALSCH

The Mother of Invention

The Legacy of Barbara Marx Hubbard and the Future of YOU

NEALE DONALD WALSCH

HAY HOUSE

Australia • Canada • Hong Kong • India
South Africa • United Kingdom • United States

First published and distributed in the United Kingdom by:
Hay House UK Ltd, 292B Kensal Rd, London W10 5BE. Tel.: (44) 20 8962 1230; Fax: (44) 20 8962 1239. www.hayhouse.co.uk

Published and distributed in the United States of America by:
Hay House, Inc., PO Box 5100, Carlsbad, CA 92018-5100. Tel.: (1) 760 431 7695 or (800) 654 5126; Fax: (1) 760 431 6948 or (800) 650 5115. www.hayhouse.com

Published and distributed in Australia by:
Hay House Australia Ltd, 18/36 Ralph St, Alexandria NSW 2015. Tel.: (61) 2 9669 4299; Fax: (61) 2 9669 4144. www.hayhouse.com.au

Published and distributed in the Republic of South Africa by:
Hay House SA (Pty), Ltd, PO Box 990, Witkoppen 2068. Tel./Fax: (27) 11 467 8904. www.hayhouse.co.za

Published and distributed in India by:
Hay House Publishers India, Muskaan Complex, Plot No.3, B-2, Vasant Kunj, New Delhi – 110 070. Tel.: (91) 11 4176 1620; Fax: (91) 11 4176 1630. www.hayhouse.co.in

Distributed in Canada by:
Raincoast, 9050 Shaughnessy St, Vancouver, BC V6P 6E5. Tel.: (1) 604 323 7100; Fax: (1) 604 323 2600

A catalogue record for this book is available from the British Library.

ISBN 978-1-8485-0302-1

Printed and bound in Great Britain by TJ International, Padstow, Cornwall.

INTRODUCTION

They say that "necessity is the mother of invention," but they're wrong. Barbara Marx Hubbard is.

And you are.

And we all are.

We are each inventing ourselves, and the life we are living, in every single moment of Now. And we are doing exactly the same for all of humanity. For as we invent ourselves individually, we do so collectively.

The act of "inventing" goes on continually. Put another way, we are *new* in every moment. We are not the same as we were before, not even for a nanosecond, nor is our species as a whole. The question is not *whether* we are changing, but *how;* not *whether* humanity is in the act of "becoming," but *what?*

In creating humanity's answer to these questions, your life *does* make a difference—and the difference it makes can be huge, if you'll *let it be.*

All of this may be a little bit difficult to believe, or at least to embrace as your Functioning Reality, but that's why this book is so perfect for you right now. It appears to be a biography, but you're soon going to find out that it is not only about someone else's life, it is about your own; that it is not only a wonderful story in which to *lose* oneself, but a wonderful way in which to *find* oneself.

The Mother of Invention is a book in which you are invited to *participate,* because the end of this story depends, in part, on you. That's why I chose to write it.

Please allow me a brief word of introduction. I am the author of 27 books on contemporary spirituality, among them the 9-book *Conversations with God* series. I believe deeply that life is creational —that is, what we are collectively experiencing is a product of what we are collectively creating. And I wanted to place before you a story that throws open the door of possibility to all of us, answering at last the question: "What can I do?" and ending at last the frustrated lament: "I'm only one person."

I wrote this book because I want you to know that ordinary, average people such as you and me can have an impact on our entire planet—and that, should we all choose to move in some of the same directions *together,* we can *really* have an impact.

This book opens that possibility for all of us, through the real-life example of a housewife and mother of five who chose to create a better world—and who is choosing to do so right now, up to this very minute.

The point of this book: If this person can do it, *we all can!*

Many people have heard of Barbara Marx Hubbard—and many people have not. I *like* the fact that she is not a household name, immediately recognizable the world over. That makes her more like us, and a wonderful *model.* A template. An outpicturing of what we *all* are—and what we are all potentialed to be.

"Potentialed" is a new word. I just made it up. I like it. It says exactly what I want it to say. I think that we all are . . . no, I *know* that we all are . . . imbued with the potential to be more than we've so far allowed ourselves to be. Further, I think that we all know it. And I think that we are all endowed with an *impulse* to move toward our highest expression of that More that we know we are.

I'm convinced that all we need is courage, and all we need to gather the courage is a model, a template, *a contemporary example, a here-and-now sample of how life could be lived* in a new way. In short, someone to inspire us.

That's where Barbara comes in. Eighty years of age at this writing, she feels that she and we are *just beginning,* that humanity is going to break *through,* not break *down,* and that we are ready to set aside our old patterns and old beliefs and old ways of being as we invent a New Human.

Barbara sees this as part of the natural evolutionary process of all sentient beings. And she believes that there is a natural Place in Time when conditions are perfect for all such beings to launch a new way of living. It is the fulcrum. It is the apogee. It is what Malcolm Gladwell calls the Tipping Point.

For humanity, that time may very well be . . . December 22, 2012.

Barbara and some of her friends are now calling this "Day One." They are inviting us to join in envisioning, planning, and creating a huge, global multimedia Satellite and Internet Experience during the days leading up to the 22nd, telling the story of our species' emergence as a new kind of human, and of *the beginning of the next cycle of evolution.*

Amidst all the anxious wondering, worried predictions, and negative speculation of many around the globe who see 2012 as an Ending, you and I are being urged by all the forces and energies of the Universe to see it as a Beginning—as Barbara sees it. Indeed, Barbara calls it "a birthing."

How has she come to this point of view? Is it realistic? Could it be true?

The answer is that the life of Barbara Marx Hubbard includes a series of spiritual encounters. Yet this is not unusual, and does not make Barbara different from most of us. I believe that each of us experience, during our time on this earth, what are called *Divine Interventions.* I define these as moments when our mind, heart, and soul are opened simultaneously. In such moments we receive at all levels—mental, emotional, and spiritual—enormous truths about life.

My observation is that most human beings (myself included) at first ignore these moments, not recognizing them for what they are. Then, when and if they do understand what is happening, they often don't know what to do about them, how to react to them, how to *use them* to their own benefit (to say nothing of using them for the benefit of humankind).

This is not our fault. We simply have not had spiritual training. Our cultures have trained us in how to use our bodies, and they have trained us in how to use our minds, but they have done very little to train us in how to interact with our souls. Indeed, and amazingly, many elements within our society don't even acknowledge the *existence* of the soul.

This is an indication of just how young our species is. Speaking metaphorically, Barbara Marx Hubbard says that we are still in the gestation period in our development and are only now about to be birthed into the cosmic community of universal beings.

How does she know this? What makes her think this is true?

It is because of those spiritual encounters in Barbara's life—three of them, to be exact. In her case, she paid attention.

As we mature, we, too, will pay attention. We will not only be able to acknowledge the existence of the part of our being from which such wisdom flows—what we might call our Higher Self—but we will also be able to *communicate* with it, receive guidance from it, and relate to it in a way that changes our lives forever.

Do we—you and I—*really* have a role to play in the process of that spiritual maturation? For ourselves and for our planet? And will we truly be able to co-create a new world, and a new way of living *in* our world, following the "end of history" in 2012? Or is this all just glib talk and wishful thinking?

Well, those are the questions to be addressed here. The answers that were given to Barbara may be the answers that can be given to you. Not all such spiritual answers come in visions or dreams or meditations. Some spiritual encounters come to us in very ordinary ways—like reading books.

So dive right in. Enjoy. Read about yourself at the same time you're reading about a perfectly normal and yet wholly remarkable woman. Rediscover yourself here.

Nay . . . *reinvent yourself.*

And all of us.

*If your life story was being put into
a book, and it was so full (as every life is) that
it would take an encyclopedia to contain it, yet for
space reasons you had to reduce it to **The 25 Most
Significant Episodes**, which episodes would
you choose, looking backward from today?*

TIMELINE IN THIS BOOK . . .

PART I: THE OUTCOME

PART II: THE PREPARATION

PART I

THE OUTCOME

"I am not alone. It is not as if I'm the only 'catalyst' on the earth. It feels as if there are many, in many different areas, undertaking many different activities."

— BARBARA MARX HUBBARD

EPISODE #25: DAY ONE, DECEMBER 22, 2012—
The Moment Barbara Marx Hubbard
Has Been Waiting for All of Her Life . . .

Imagine this day with me, will you? Visualize it in your mind. It is a very interesting time on planet Earth, and this day, in particular, is a day that some people thought would never arrive. Others thought it would arrive all right, but they thought it would be a picture of global chaos when it did.

These were the 2012 Doomsdayers, a group of apparently well-intentioned but clearly not very well-informed people living in various parts of the world who felt that they had correctly interpreted certain Signs and Wonders (among them, the Mayan Long Count calendar) as indicating that the day *before* this day—December 21, 2012—would be the End of History. Now envision this day, "the day after," in your imagination.

Watch as a dozen technicians scurry about a large stage in a major auditorium in Phoenix, Arizona. Powered by portable solar panels, huge megawatt klieg lights are juiced and aimed as long-armed boom mikes are moved to markings on the floor. Television

cameras (a slew of them) are rolled into place; and colorfully cos-
tumed actors, singers, and dancers have heard the ancient call of
stage managers everywhere—"Places everyone. Places!"—and are
taking their positions as an audience numbering well over a thousand is finding its seats.

Around the world, people gather in front of computer screens,
television screens, movie-theater screens, and in some cases, huge
stretch-screens set up in sundry and sometimes unexpected loca-
tions, like the middle of dusty fields or the front of church halls or
the 50-yard line of football stadiums. And this, too—all of it—is
powered by portable solar sources. Close attention has been paid
to the ecological footprint of this worldwide event to avoid over-
use of precious resources.

A few moments pass, and then a petite but not frail woman of
some years—in her early 80s from appearances—steps to a stand-
alone microphone in a small soundproof booth off stage right. She
adjusts a headset over her snow-white hair, tapping with antici-
pating fingers the music stand on which she has placed a reading
script, and glancing at a video monitor directly in front of her.

It is 7 P.M. where she is standing, but it is other times and even
another day in other parts of the world—and she knows that her
voice is about to be heard in every major city on the globe and
most of the smaller ones.

See, in your inner vision, all of this. A live orchestra is huddled
in a pit just below the front of the stage, its members responding
instantly and with beautiful precision to a sharp baton wave from
its conductor. A stirring overture begins.

The woman clears her throat; presses the ON switch in a panel
to her left; and waits for a cue from this telecast's director, en-
sconced in a glassed-in booth high above and behind the audience. A burst of graphic special effects splays across the video
monitor.

The majestic music dips under. "Go," the director intones.

"And so," the woman begins in a voice soft and gentle, yet
surprisingly firm, "we've come to this. Gloriously, wondrously, remarkably, magnificently, we've come to this. . . ."

She pauses for dramatic effect. Then . . .
"Welcome to Day One."

Create This Along with Me

Continue your visioning. Or, envision along with me. . . .

I see the curtain majestically rise as a multimedia display ignites a 50-foot expanse of reflective fabric upstage. A pictorial montage captures the Journey of Humankind from the beginning to the present moment in a series of rapid-fire projections, while an eruption of dancers in black and white enhance the on-screen images with breathtaking pantomime ballet.

The cameras gulp it all in and convert it into digitalized signals, instantly sped across the globe. A worldwide multimedia satellite and Internet event featuring live feeds from 27 nations and viewed by more than 100 million people is under way. So, too, is a New Future for the inhabitants of planet Earth.

Can you imagine this with me? That last part is the most important. Whether it is introduced with a huge stage spectacular on worldwide television, found on the pages of an exciting and inspiring book, or discovered through the writings and teachings of a woman who inspires people wherever she goes, we are talking here about a New Future for the inhabitants of our planet.

Hold *this* in your mind's eye. For this is the plan—this is the vision.

It is a vision not specifically of a collaborative stage spectacular, not simply of a "show," but of a huge shift in humanity's experience itself. A shift in humanity's experience *of* itself. And what many thought would be the End of Time turns out to be the beginning of the best time that human beings have ever had. This shift is made possible in part by a new technology that opens the door for global, nonlinear, exponential interaction around what's working.

Our joint experience upon the earth may not reach that level in the moments of December 22, 2012, nor in the weeks or months immediately afterward, nor even in the first few years following this date—but it does begin to manifest at that time.

This will always be remembered as The Beginning, the moment when you, and all the people of the planet, decided jointly (and for the first time on such a scale) to reach for a higher purpose; a greater calling; a more loving and harmonious way of living; a grander notion of who we are and who we could be; and a more elevated, unified, *intentioned* expression of Life itself.

Let me say that again, because sometimes the best and most exciting ideas are lost in the reading. *I believe that December 22, 2012, will always be remembered as The Beginning:* the moment when you, and all the people of the planet, decided jointly (and for the first time on such a scale) to reach for . . .

- A higher purpose
- A greater calling
- A more loving and harmonious way of living
- A grander notion of who we are and who we could be
- A more elevated, unified, *intentioned* expression of Life itself

At the center of it all, at the core of this true "birthing," stands Barbara Marx Hubbard—a woman who has been called the Mother of Invention—earphones wrapped around her head, script in hand, and just the smallest tear slowly channeling its way from her left eye to her chin. Barbara Marx Hubbard's life mission has been accomplished. This is the 25th of the 25 Most Significant Episodes of her Life—and that tear is liquid happiness.

Who is this woman? Well, you may or may not have heard of her up to this moment, but she is someone whom you will certainly want to know, because she's your midwife. And mine. And all of ours.

🌿 🌿 🌿

2

EPISODE #15 (OUT OF ORDER):
THE CONTACT, AUGUST 23, 2002—
Ten Years and Four Months Before Day One . . .

Barbara Marx Hubbard is using the couch in a unique way. She is neither sitting on it nor lying on it, but rather, doing a bit of both. She is sitting at one end and facing the other, her legs outstretched before her.

It is six in the morning. She is in a small room in the back of a house in Montecito, California. It is a dark room, especially so at this hour. There's not much in it, but given its size, there couldn't be. A battered desk, piles of old papers in boxes . . . the place feels almost like a storage room. The couch isn't really a couch, but an old daybed with a headboard on both sides, covered with a musty throw.

With all of that, the room is comfortable enough. And quiet. Most of all, quiet. And that's perfect for Barbara on this morning, because a lot of wondering and a bit of frustration are traveling the avenues of her mind these days. Most of all, she is yearning to "make contact."

Barbara knows there is something more to be experienced in this lifetime. She knows there is something more for her "out there." She may not know exactly what is awaiting her, or where "out there" is, but she knows that both exist.

She is sure of it—and has been since she was a child. Yet for years Barbara has been so galvanized by a social-evolution movement that she herself had helped to create, that she almost felt as if she had no "self" at all. She certainly had never created a space in which to nurture herself. So yes, this musty, dusty, crusty back room would do nicely for now. It wasn't even her house, but here it was, and here she was, and that's how *it* was on this summer morning.

Opening a Door of Possibility

A few nights before, Barbara had attended a lecture by Nassim Haramein, a brilliant physicist who is exploring the unified-field theory and who is also the founder of The Resonance Project. Haramein pries open a door of possibility in Barbara's mind, confirming everything that she has believed—and doing so with data that is all scientifically based, which impresses her enormously.

Nassim Haramein states with absolute certainty that we've been contacted by highly evolved beings from other places or dimensions in the Universe. It is this contact for which Barbara yearns.

And so it is that at six o'clock on this morning, Barbara is meditating. Half sitting, half lying on the old daybed, her eyes closed, her journaling notebook in her lap, she is vaguely aware of a small terrier at her feet.

The dog always comes around and plunks down in this same spot whenever Barbara is meditating. Perhaps he picks up on the innately inviting energy of such moments. For whatever reason, he's there again. They're both in this tiny room near the back of the house where Barbara is spending a few days with her beloved other.

Sidney Lanier and Barbara have been walking hand in hand for nearly 20 years. They are pals, lovers, partners on The Journey, and companions in The Quest. They live in separate places because this is what works, and they spend days on end just "hanging out" with each other often. This is one of those days.

Sidney is asleep and Barbara is wide awake, meditating a room away. The home is not Sidney's, and neither is the dog. Both belong to a friend with whom Sidney is staying. The friend is an architect and muralist who travels a lot on business. The house (and the dog) frequently need watching over, so the arrangement works out well for both men. And when Sidney's friend is away, Barbara comes over for a few days—which works out well for Sidney.

And so, Barbara is sitting/lying on the daybed, the household terrier her silent companion. *Give me contact,* Barbara is urging with the voiceless voice of her mind.

Give me contact.

And Then There Was Light

Barbara is silent now, breathing softly. Waiting. Eyes closed, not moving at all, but breathing, breathing, breathing . . . and waiting.

Then . . . a feeling.

She is filled with it. And transfixed.

She would describe it later as "a vibrant field of Light that was ecstatic, joyful, beyond the field of physicality yet somehow connected to my own essential being . . . a continuation of my own self at a different frequency."

In her mind's eye, she can see a kind of "being" materialize. It is an inner visual experience, a "presence" that she later speaks of as "nonlocal and yet totally present here-and-now—very much like those UFO stories in which beings can materialize and dematerialize."

Barbara is intrigued by the experience of *nonlocality* and yet *connectivity* through a kind of *unity*.

She stays with the experience for a while—and then, for no apparent reason but very much all of a sudden, she is startled by a realization: this seemingly "other" being is *herself.*

Of course it was totally present here-and-now! Was Barbara herself not sitting/lying right here on the daybed? Yet she *felt* "nonlocal," and she was! For her consciousness had *expanded* beyond all the limits of her body.

Who is the new kind of Self? Barbara wonders. *Maybe,* she thinks to herself, *I'm mutating.*

Keeping her eyes closed, she sits very still. The sense that has come over her is enlarged and "like a nontangible Presence" from which she gets "clairaudience, with a verbal download and a feeling of vibration," she tells Sidney later.

"It felt like I was a being of light . . . so joyful, so ecstatic!"

Then she "hears" (Feels? Experiences?) a Voice:

Keep your intention on me.

She cocks her head and listens for more. And there is more.

The Voice says: *This is the next stage of evolution for Barbara.*

Now she knows. The God presence is within her, around her, and beyond her. She feels as if there are no limits to her own body. She watches herself melt into being one with everyone and experiences herself traveling throughout the Universe and sitting there on the daybed at the same time. Her body feels light, and she begins to move her legs to make certain that she is still there and still has control of her physical self.

"Woof!"

The dog lets out a bark. Sitting there at Barbara's feet, he is startled by her sudden movement.

"Woof! Woof!" He won't stop.

The moment has been interrupted. Barbara quiets the terrier down, hoping that Sidney hasn't already been awakened. He has not. He could sleep through a train traversing the bedroom. So she takes out her journal and writes.

For two straight hours . . . without interruption.

She is, she finds, taking dictation. And the Voice—her own inner voice, her own higher voice—has a lot to say.

Getting It All Down

Barbara is writing at breakneck speed, scribbling words without thinking. She has begun a Secret Journal. She is clear that she cannot show this to anyone. Not now. Not yet. Perhaps, not ever.

Who would believe it? How to explain it?

She is about to find out. Sidney is up. Moseying around the place, he finds his lover in the postage-stamp back room.

"Mornin'," he chirps, looking in.

"Oh, Sidney, I've got to talk with you!"

Her companion smiles. He has been here before. It is rare that Barbara doesn't have something infinitely interesting to say. He loves her for this—rather, he adores her.

"Lemme get some coffee."

"Hurry, darling, hurry."

Sidney hurries.

He is a godsend. But then again, he has been for 20 years. *Who would believe it? How to explain it?* Why, Sidney would believe it, of course! And he would require very little explanation! Barbara tries out her theory, the words tumbling out of her mouth, one on top of the other.

"This is the next stage of our evolution . . . the end of old religions. I met a universal being, but it didn't feel like contact with an extraterrestrial . . . it felt like contact with my own greater self . . . I feel I'm now part of the vast Universe of selves."

Again Sidney smiles. But it is not an indulgent smile, not a "That's nice, dear" smile. He heard her. Absolutely. Completely. And he "got it." At once. He was tracking right with her. And, of course, he wanted to know more.

"Tell me everything you learned, everything you heard. I want to hear it all."

"I've *got* it all!" Barbara beams. "Right here! I've been writing in my journal for hours!"

"Can you share it?"

"Yes, with *you* I can! Listen!"

She turns the pages back to the beginning.

"Listen to *this*. . . ."

🌾 🌾 🌾

11

3.

Sidney is all ears. Barbara begins to read from her journal, announcing beforehand: "This is what was 'dictated' to me this morning. . . ."

Of course, the first reaction she had to the joyous feeling of ecstasy that came over her several hours earlier, and to the overall sense of a "presence" that was local and nonlocal at the same time, was to ask, "Who are you?"

She received this response:

> *I am a Guardian of the Gateway, the passageway to the next stage of evolution. You came through a stellar gate with the knowledge needed for this time.*
>
> *You have had the fortitude to hold the space for the template, as you call it, since the bomb fell over 50 years ago.*

Barbara knew exactly what that statement made reference to. There had been a moment when, as a young woman decades earlier, she innocently asked President Dwight David Eisenhower, in a private conversation in the Oval Office, a question he could not answer. From that point on, she knew she had to do something—*something*—for the world. If even *the President of the United States* didn't have an answer . . .

But just what she could do wasn't clear then—nor did it become clear for many years. Now the pieces of a lifelong puzzle were coming together. Barbara had the answer. And she'd had it all along.

She wrote in her journal: *What should I be writing here?*

She received the reply:

You should be writing exactly what you are writing. Take from your writings inspired by us, your daily inspiration.

And the outcome? The purpose?

The first reward is union with ME—Essence. The second reward is when integrated Essence/ego experiences the Kingdom of Heaven within, not losing all sense of person, but as a Universal Person unbound by local self.

The next sentence stopped Barbara when it first came through, and it's stopping her again now. She takes a deep breath. Sidney, with his charmingly childlike eagerness, is impatient. "Well? What else did It say? Is that it?"

"Oh, no, there is much more. Over two hours' worth."

"Great! Read on. What did It say next?"

Barbara shifts slightly in her chair. "It said . . ." and then she reads the statement aloud: *You are a demonstration of a Universal Human.*

Now both of them become quiet. The words hang in the air between them. Finally, Barbara speaks.

"Sidney, I don't feel like this. I've felt glimpses of this on and off through the years, but I don't feel that I've attained this. And my thoughts, my feelings about that, must have been clear and must have been 'read' by whoever it was that was dictating this to me, because here is what was said next:"

To fully incarnate, you will now experience not the Rose Chamber of Union of the Human and the Divine, but the Cosmic

Oneness with Source within you as an incarnate human, fully human/fully Divine—as a new norm.

"So," Sidney began, slowly, "you're going to be a model for the rest of us."

Barbara's reply was quick and certain. "No," she said. "That's not it at all. I can't do that, and I'm not being asked to do that."

"But It said—"

"Wait. When It talked of my being a 'new norm,' it immediately added . . . "

Not an exemplar, but rather, a catalyst for so many others who are right at the threshold of their own emergence.

"That I can do," Barbara allowed. "An 'exemplar' I'm not; a 'catalyst' I can be. It is what I was *meant* to be, and I'm not alone. It's not as if I'm the only catalyst on the earth. It feels as if there are many, in many different areas, undertaking many different activities."

"I agree with you," Sidney confirms. "This *is* what you were meant to be. What do you have to do next?"

"I was told that. I was given specific instructions." Barbara turns the page in her journal and reads again:

I ask you now to experience the Kingdom within, in this full, whole incarnation as a young Universal Human.

Then she reads to Sidney her own words, entered in response:

As a Guardian of the Gate, guide me in this experience. I have been up to now so directed in my mission that I've rarely, if ever, experienced the inner peace.

Now let me experience, as a steady state, the Inner Kingdom—it is from this still point that a convergence center is offered, I know.

For you, beloved, as an Earth-born Universal Human, the step requires a direct love affair, like you once had with the risen Christ.

Barbara also knew what this referred to. There was a time, years earlier, when she experienced a direct union with Christ—a sense of Oneness she would never forget. But this moment, right now, was different.

This love is with a specific Being who is your actual partner in the process. I am beyond you—yet so close. This falling upward in love is the attraction that you need now.

Yes, that's what's required now! Barbara knew it down to her bones. It was about "falling upward in love." But upward beyond even the Christed One? With *whom*, then? Falling in love with *whom*?

The Kingdom for a Homo Universalis during the birth process on a planet is different from that which Jesus outlined 2,000 years ago. That was then; this is now.

Now is the birth process on planet Earth. It is vital that you embody, grow into, and become a Being on the Other Side of the Veil—alive, tangible, and real to your Self—to help bring other people through.

To do so, you cannot be alone either on this Earth or beyond; but for your next step, you need to be with at least one other who has already made it through in another planetary sequence.

That is why I am now coming directly to you.

Once again, Barbara stopped reading. She reached for a tissue from a nearby box. She dabbed at her eyes and daubed a sniffle. This time, Sidney controlled his impatience. He understood how meaningful this was to Barbara—and how challenging it was for her to share it, even with him.

Presently, Barbara continued.

I want you to clear your mind of all tasks. You now know The Plan for you. It is now indelibly imprinted, and it will unfold. You do not need to keep reviewing it mentally to hold it. Let it set like a photograph in a darkroom, undisturbed.

Put your attention on Me, your partner already on the Other Side.

So there it was, the guidance and instruction. But still the question remained: Who is the "partner" on the "Other Side"? Who is this being with whom Barbara is invited to "fall upward in love" even more than Christ?

For the answer, Barbara was being invited to . . .

Go in your mind's eye . . . into the future. It is the future from the human perspective, but it is the present from the perspective of those of us who are already here.

Barbara explained to Sidney that she did just that, hours earlier when she was doing the original writing in her journal. She closed her eyes and tried to imagine the future in order to identify her partner from the Other Side.

"I didn't know what to expect," she told him. "I had no preconceived idea. Then, suddenly, I experienced contact *with my own Self.*"

Sidney's eyebrows shot up. Barbara went on: "Not with the risen Christ, nor an extraterrestrial, but *my own self, evolved.* Then, these words came to me:"

I combine all the characteristics that are incipient in you full grown.

Just imagine yourself as a fully embodied Universal Human, living in an Earth space universal environment, able to resonate in a nonlocal universe.

Imagine your body fully sensitive to your intention with continuity of consciousness through many bodies.

Imagine you are interacting freely with others—like Me— who have gone before. Experience fulfilling your mission on Earth; the shared planetary birth experience as a Universal Human, at your own next stage of development, with the rapturous experience of what used to be called gods.

Feel beloved by the Beloved, and experience the Presence as Who You Are.

Barbara looked up and smiled. "Well, I asked for it," she chuckled. "I said I wanted 'contact.' I was told I had to fall 'upward in love.' I just didn't know that it was going to be with *me!*"

❧ ❧ ❧

We'll return to that fascinating dialogue later in this book, and as it continues, we'll find that it contains some remarkable information. More important, we'll all have a chance to experience the dialogue as if it were an exchange with *us*. (Because, in a larger sense, it *is*.)

Yet right now, I'd like to lay a bit more of a foundation for the story we've just begun.

The lady whose life we're exploring here says that the human species is going through a birthing process. She adds that every one of us is part of that. If this is true (and I believe that, by the end of this book, you'll see and agree that it is), it would be wonderful, as in any birthing, to have a loving, caring, knowing midwife present.

This is a role that Barbara Marx Hubbard models spectacularly well, and that is why it is so perfect for us to now know all about her and the unique role she is playing in nurturing our planetary emergence.

The fascinating aspect of this collective Birthing of a New Humanity is that we are all *both the parent and the offspring*. We are the Creator and the Created. We are *all* the Mother of Invention, and we are The Invention itself. In a sense, we are our *own* midwife.

We are reinventing *ourselves* in a global (dare I say, *universal*) process by which humanity will emerge as a new and magnificent form of our particular species of sentient beings—a form that only loves, and never again hates; that only shares, and never again hoards; that only heals, and never again hurts; and that only births and rebirths itself in ever new and more glorious ways, and never again kills.

If we hold and sustain that vision—if those of us who are connected here, via this book, use this book itself as *causal art* (a book, painting, photograph, poem, play, or movie that inspires and *causes* an outcome to occur)—then the *manifestation* of the vision on a global scale can begin in earnest on December 22 of that much-talked-about year, 2012.

The 2012 Phenomenon

Yes, yes, here we go again . . . more 2012 "stuff." Except this "stuff" isn't about predictions of the end of the world, the collapse of our social systems at every level, the return to caveman days, or whatever else the Purveyors of Doom have put out there.

Now make no mistake—there are going to be a lot of changes. But not changes for the worse. No. They'll be changes for the *better;* changes in the way we relate to each other, changes in the way we "do" politics and economics and medicine and science and technology and entertainment and sports and education and religion and just about *every aspect of human life.*

They will be changes in our social mores, belief systems, and cultural constructions in everything from livelihood to marriage to sexuality to parenting and to what we label "good," "fun," "joyful," and "loving"; and what we label as *not* that.

Yes, humanity's ideas, actions, intentions, and results are going to change—and change mightily—in the years just ahead. And we're all going to be playing a huge role in the creation of that.

Unless we aren't.

We don't *have* to play a role. We can just sit back and watch it all happen. But we will certainly be invited to. In fact, we *are* being invited to. By Life itself—right now.

So what are you reading here, anyway? Is this a biography? Well, yes and no. It's more of a *uniography*. What in the world is that? Wait, you'll see. For this *is* the personal history of an extraordinary person, but there's more to the story. . . .

History, Herstory, Ourstory

It's a most extraordinary thing, really, a person's life. And every life means more than what the one who is living it usually knows. Yet there are some people who *do* know—who are very clear and aware—even as each moment is being lived. These are human beings who have a sense of the true meaning of their days upon the earth.

This book is about just such a person, and it is about how *you* can become such a person—or be even *more* of that if you already *are* that.

Whenever I talk with Barbara Marx Hubbard, I have the feeling that she's mainlining the aggregate genius and the sum total of all wisdom in the Universe.

Really.

Over the decade and a half that I've known her, I've never, ever had a dull conversation with her; never, ever heard a silly or ill-thought-out idea from her; never, ever came across any piece of writing from her that didn't sparkle with a special kind of brilliance, wrapped as it is in the effervescent bubbling of one who Simply and Joyously Knows.

Now you may think that I'm exaggerating about this woman, but when you finish reading this book, you'll know that I'm not. Not even a little. But let's be clear about something. We would be making a huge mistake if we allowed ourselves to think that Barbara is all that I've just said she is because she is somehow "better equipped" than most other people. If that were true, there would be little point in your reading this book—and no point in my writing it. I have no interest in writing "just another biography," and I'm sure you have enough to do right now without reading one of those. If I'm going to take the time to write a book, and if you're going to take the time to read it, it's going to have to *bring something,* yes?

Yes. I don't have enough days left in my life to just ramble on about somebody for the sake of simply telling her story, however unusual or extraordinary. I want every word that I write to have something to do with *me* and with *you.* So let me promise you early on that *this* story has a lot to do with *our* story.

Not Your Ordinary Biography

Perhaps you've noticed as we get deeper into this book that it is being written in a somewhat unusual "voice" and style. Most books of this kind are presented in a much more detached, third-person narrative voice. I can't adopt that. First of all, I'm not that kind of writer. I have to come from my own personal experience or I lose interest. Second, I've known Barbara Marx Hubbard for way too many years to somehow "detach" myself from my subject here and speak to you about her in a distant, objective voice.

And finally, I don't *want* to be objective about what we're going to be exploring, because, as I keep saying over and over again, we will not be simply examining a person's life here—we're *applying* what we *learn* about that life *to our own.*

We're also going to be hearing some of the most exciting news the human race has received in a very long time, and I can't be aloof about that. I don't even want to try.

So my own voice is going to be very "present" here. I'm throwing myself *into* this story, making myself a part *of* it, not simply telling it.

(Just to warn you.)

People Who Enliven Our Lives

You know what I've discovered? Everybody has something to learn from everybody else. We are all each other's teacher. And it's especially nice to meet people who not only know this, but who consciously and enthusiastically fill the role of teacher in our lives, even while they are students in their own. They enliven life itself, moving as they do through the minutes of their every day with actions, choices, and words supercharged with Conscious Intention and driven by Purpose.

When I first met Barbara Marx Hubbard, I realized that I had come across just such a person—someone from whom I could learn, and from whom I would benefit, for the rest of my life. Even after she is gone.

Barbara belongs to that special category of folks who know that their lives were meant to touch others in an important way. Indeed, to *change* the lives of others. In fact (why beat around the bush?), to *benefit the whole of humanity.*

Now that might seem like a grandiose notion, but I've had the experience that those who embrace such a notion are not grandiose at all, but are nearly always humbled by such a thought—if not actually *burdened* by it. Who wants to walk around feeling that the whole of humanity is expecting something momentous from you?

Yet if you feel that way, you feel that way. *Something is calling to you,* and you couldn't ignore it if you wanted to.

I have a notion that this is a feeling with which you, yourself, may be familiar. It is a calling to create something, to experience something, to *be* something greater. It is the calling of evolution itself, the deep inner impulse, the Grand Invitation of Divinity to rejoin It, to know It, to become It.

Do you know why I have this notion about you? *Because you are reading this book.* You wouldn't have been drawn to this if there wasn't something deep inside of you saying, "Here! Here is the invitation you have been waiting for! This is not just *history.* Yes, this is Barbara's story, but it's not just '*herstory.*' This is '*yourstory.*' Read it—and then choose to be part of the global Birthing of Humanity."

*** *** ***

5.

Just for a second, let's go "back to the future." Imagine again that it is the 22nd day of the closing month of 2012, and imagine that it has been magnificent. All over the world people have gathered in front of their computers; televisions; neighborhood movie theaters; and in some outlying villages, in front of large projection screens in church halls, public buildings, and even in dusty fields.

They've been waiting for this moment for a long time. Many have believed that on December 21 something horrific was going to happen. They were not sure what—the earth tilting on its axis, a large meteor striking the planet, a gigantic quake and tsunami altering an entire globe's landscape—but they seemed resigned and ready for the worst. With this cataclysmic event would come the catastrophic collapse of our political, financial, and social systems. The world, in short, would be thrown into chaos.

Much of this speculation has been based on an interpretation of the Mayan Long calendar, which some say has predicted that on these very days, the human race would reach the End of History.

And so the world stood watch as the Big Day approached. Not everyone, it should be noted, watched with fear or apprehension. Many didn't embrace the doomsday scenarios that flew around the blogosphere, filled newspapers and magazines, and even served as the basis of a major motion picture released a few years prior.

Some even felt, going into these days, a wonderful sense of exhilaration, joyful expectation, and even of *participation* in the creation of a glorious New Tomorrow, having read the 2011 best-selling book *The Mother of Invention,* in which the events of these very days were anticipated and described.

That book helped create the energy for the collective forward leap that has been taken by humanity in the last 48 hours, for it joined with many people and organizations in rallying people all over the world to the cause. It has been the Cause of Co-Creation, and it has been a remarkable occurrence, all the more stunning because of how accurately these developments were predicted.

True, the book didn't describe every single aspect, down to the smallest detail, with unerring accuracy, but—given that it was written two and a half years in advance—it proved to be astonishingly prescient.

The Entire World Is Co-Creating— for the First Time Ever at This Level

The most remarkable thing about what is happening today is that even before the day is finished, thousands of people from all over the world have already joined in the creation of our glorious new tomorrow by posting their thoughts, best ideas, insights, and specific data about programs and projects that are already working at the local level into the "Synergy Engine"—a unique and special place on the Internet.

This may well be the first time in the history of our species that so many individuals have offered so many ideas in so short a period of time. But there is something else radically new about the Synergy Engine. It does more than herald a new era of global collaboration. It ushers in a new era of global *coherence.*

Of course, we've had global communication now for quite some time, but we've never before seen such *organized* global collaboration: communication with such a clear intention and specific purpose that it produces *coherence*. That is because never before yesterday has humanity had anything like the Synergy Engine.

The Engine integrates as a *core social function* the first Internet technology the world has ever seen that's capable of providing a scientifically validated reflection of the individual and collective (energetic, heart) coherence of everyone engaging it, encouraging an even greater coherence through awareness.

The designers of the Synergy Engine recognize that it is not, and will not be, enough if it simply brings together all of the world's wonderful ideas and solutions. It must also bring us to a new *reason* for *applying* those solutions, a new awareness of who we are in relation to each other, a new consciousness about Life itself, the purpose of this experience, our place in it, and our True Identity. This awareness is what coherence invites, and has created.

Because of this, yesterday truly was, as Barbara Marx Hubbard declared during the worldwide telecast, "Day One."

Since the publication of *The Mother of Invention,* the world has been waiting for today's unveiling of the Synergy Engine, said to be the most powerful planetary networking platform ever created for the World Wide Web. The book promised that "everyone, everywhere on Earth" would be invited to place their creative gifts, their projects, their search for teammates and partners in the Synergy Engine . . . and so they have.

The Engine, as the book explained, is modeled on a wheel (the "Wheel of Co-Creation," Barbara calls it) that is fully programmed to receive hundreds of thousands of postings from anyone with access to a computer. (Even people without such access have been invited to mail, fax, or even text in their entries, which are posted by a worldwide staff of volunteers working 24 hours a day, 7 days a week, to capture, monitor, and enter the data.)

The postings are being placed in whatever section seems to be the best "fit." The "spokes" of the Wheel divide it into many areas: Governance, Education, Technology, Medicine, Science, Communication, Culture and the Arts, Spirituality, Economics and

Commerce, Community Building, Transportation, Planning and Zoning, Health and Human Services, Money/Banking/Finance, Parenting, and so forth. The list goes on and on, covering every major area of human endeavor.

The idea is not to "silo" human activity by separating it into discrete spokes or "specialties," but just the opposite: to create a mechanism that vividly reveals and demonstrates that it is the *interconnection,* the *intersection,* the *cross-discipline,* the *cross-sectoral interaction* that creates Whole System Synergy.

The purpose of the Wheel is to give humans all across the planet a place to share their best innovations and their most wonderful ideas about how to make every one of these areas work more efficiently, effectively, compassionately, and humanely for the human species. Its function is to exponentially increase the interaction of people who are creating "what's working," and to scale solutions globally. It is a matrix that connects what is emerging, positive, and loving.

Some of the ideas that are being posted have already been tried and proven to be successful—although on a localized scale, not yet globally. Others have been fully developed and planned for widespread application and are now ready for on-the-ground implementation. Still others are in the gestation stage, but even this sneak preview will reveal that they offer breathtaking promise. And, of course, such a preview will garner much-needed entrepreneurial backing and managerial support.

In other words, *collaboration.*

Synergistic Partnerships.

Across the globe.

The result brings together people who didn't even know that those ideas, projects, proposals, solutions, and innovations existed until the launching of the Synergy Engine.

The text of *The Mother of Invention* promised that *all* the ideas would be placed in the Engine, on the Wheel, like an engine of evolution, without judgment or prejudicial comment, in a true celebration of human creativity and compassion; and that is exactly what has happened.

To use Barbara's birth analogy, it is like the moment when a newborn baby's nervous system first "connects" after the panic of birth. The infant takes its first coordinated breath, opens its eyes . . . and hopefully, smiles. It has made it through the birth canal. It's newly born, with vast new capacities that are already present, ready to be developed.

Those capacities are emergent in the planetary system now, Barbara knows, and the Day One experience is designed to serve as an evolutionary catalyst to assist the newly connected universal species—humanity—to realize its immense creativity and potential as a whole.

The plan—set in motion two years earlier in 2010 by people all over the world—was for the global telecast to be covering the "birth" live, as a shared experience that would be felt, seen, and manifested in action. And that's exactly what happened yesterday during the global event, when the Synergy Engine was officially unveiled in a remarkable ceremony in which representatives of every nation on Earth simultaneously pressed symbolic ON buttons in their nation's capital cities.

"This is our birthing," they declared one by one, each in their own native language. "Our creativity is being turned on collectively. Having birthed together, we move forward as brothers and sisters for the whole of humanity."

How It Has Been Working So Far

Today, just hours after the Synergy Engine revved up, 73,248 entries have been posted. Some are two-line suggestions; some are treatise-length descriptions. All are there for the world to see— and already, collaborations and connections are being made.

City councils, county commissioners, and state legislators all over the United States, and their counterparts throughout the world, are at this hour screening the ideas for better governance. Corporation chieftains and financial experts are looking at the ideas surrounding business and commerce and economics. Members of the clergy of every major religion have already announced a global conference to review the postings on spirituality—and on solving the world's problems using spiritual means. And in every other area of the Wheel, experts are reviewing the earliest postings.

"We've demonstrated that anyone anywhere can place his or her story in the larger story of our birth," a statement released by the Day One organizers this afternoon said.

"The world is fascinated by the graphic that indicates that wherever individuals enter the Wheel of Co-Creation, they help turn the Wheel. The Synergy Engine is now working to connect them. We have some live stories coming in from people throughout the world. It is their love story we are telling. *Our Story.* Everyone's! It is the 'new' news of what is breaking through out of what is breaking down.

"The Synergy Engine is now, in the blink of an eye, connecting People and Projects and Promise. This is a giant step for humankind, producing Potential where once there were only Problems; Planning and Progress where once there were only Poverty and Pain; and creating at long last the very real Possibility of Planetary Peace."

Reaching into Space?

One of the most exciting parts of the global Day One event originating in Phoenix yesterday was the moment when astronauts from each of the space-traveling nations read a joint statement: "We reach out together into space," they said, "as we seek new sources of knowledge, energy, space, and life itself, even as we are further connecting as one body here on Earth."

And so, our "planetary nervous system," as Barbara Marx Hubbard described it yesterday, has begun to connect. Our Internet and Global Brain—demonstrated here as the Synergy Engine—will continue to invite people to enter their visions and projects in the Wheel of Co-Creation.

As the Day One organizers and producers said yesterday, "This is a *live, participatory process.*"

NOT WHAT SOME EXPECTED, BUT WHAT EVERYONE HOPED

Internet news pages and hard-copy newspapers around the world ran headlines pretty close to the one above, taken from CNN Online News.

And so, as Ms. Marx Hubbard said when the final evening's spectacular program began last night, we've come to this.

Gloriously, wondrously, remarkably, magnificently . . . we've come to this.

ℐ ℐ ℐ

REFLECTIONS & EXPLORATIONS

Seeing Beyond the Horizon

Beginning with this chapter, I'm going to pause in the narrative of *The Mother of Invention* every so often to reflect on the times just described and explore the benefit that Barbara Marx Hubbard's experience can offer all of us. In this way, this book becomes more than just Barbara's story; it becomes part of your story and mine, a teaching tool for all of us and a reminder of how things are.

For instance, examining the previous narrative, we are reminded that . . .

. . . a vision is only limited by the horizon of our sight.

When you allow yourself to see beyond the horizon—to know that the horizon itself is not the end of anything, but merely the place where time and space curve—then straight-line thinking stops, visions become expansive, possibilities become enormous, futures become wondrous, events unfurl magnificently, and life responds to your calling.

Life is here to serve us; we are not here to serve life. Yet life cannot serve us if we don't know what we are here to do. And we can't truly know what we are here to do until and unless we truly understand who we really are.

If we imagine that we are simple beings—perhaps not much more, in the end, than biological incidents—then we will have one set of ideas about what we are here to do. At the top of that list, we might imagine that we are here to survive. And then, perhaps, if we are "believers," we might imagine that we are here to learn our lessons, behave well, and find our way back "home." Then we do the best we can for ourselves and our loved ones while we are here, to get through it all having lived a "good life" and, hopefully, having harmed no one—or at least very few, and in relatively small ways.

All of this may be good enough. Goodness knows, this is the way 95 percent of the world's people move through their lives. If, on the other hand, we imagine that we are more than simple beings—that we are Aspects of the Divine, Universal Beings directly connected to, and one with, the Universal Self—we will have another set of ideas about what we are here to do.

So the central questions to examine closely as we reflect upon the 2012 Day One event, the birthing of humanity, and this portion of the life of Barbara Marx Hubbard, are these: *Who am I? Where am I? Why am I here?* and *What am I intending to do here?*

We will explore these questions deeply on the pages ahead, through the telling of more and more of Barbara's story.

Enjoy.

≈ ≈ ≈

Barbara Marx Hubbard has heard that *calling* I just spoke of. And I'm not talking about the dialogue she had in that mystical moment of Contact in August 2002. I'm talking about an inner calling, a deep inner impulse she has felt her entire life.

That is what caused her to conceptualize and inspire the creation of the Synergy Engine, and it's that calling that has ultimately brought her to the planning of, and participation in, the Day One event on December 22, 2012—which just happens (by noncoincidence) *to be her birthday.*

Barbara has heard that calling and has felt it for more than 70 years, in one form or another. She is past 80 now and has been living with this feeling since somewhere around the age of 8. And right now, as this is being written, she's reaching the fulfillment of that calling.

Isn't that great? Right there is a fabulous lesson.

Don't ever give up. Keep at it, whatever is calling to you. Even if you're 80, never give up. Pour everything you've got into it, and take everything it's got out of it. Then you'll never, ever feel like saying: "What's this life all about?" "Why am I here?" or "I know I'm supposed to be making a difference; I just want to get on with it!"

That's how Barbara felt when she was little. Then she began *activating the calling.* I'm going to explain how she did that, because it's something that many of the rest of us have wanted to do. As I said, we, too, have had the feeling of "wanting to make a difference" and of sometimes just not being able to "get on with it."

That kind of feeling can gnaw away at you. It can stop you from doing *anything,* out of utter frustration. Or, it can push you into doing *everything,* out of utter determination.

Many people go in the first direction. Barbara went in the second. And any of us can go in the second even if we've found ourselves frustrated and stopped. Barbara, too, felt "stopped" in her life—more than once—but she never let the feeling take over forever. She made whatever changes she had to (including changing her entire *identity,* in terms of her role in the world); and that's what is most important and inspiring about her story.

Just Like You

I said earlier that Barbara is no different from the rest of us, and she isn't. She's a regular person. Ah, but she's acting in a very irregular way—a way that she believes will become "regular" for *us* in a short period of time.

This will happen after that birthing I talked about; after you and I and the rest of the earth's people are birthed as a co-creative, universal species. But that birthing is not guaranteed. The process is not yet complete, and the outcome is anything but assured. And so, we must be careful.

As Barbara puts it: "Like a baby just before birth, we will destroy ourselves if we continue to grow in the womb.

"Thus, we are being moved *out* of the womb of limited, self-centered consciousness and planet-boundedness and into a new and expanded life—first on this Earth, then in the solar system, and ultimately, beyond."

It may seem strange for you to suddenly keep hearing about what is happening with humanity right now as a "birth." We have, after all, been around for quite a while. Yet when new life emerges in the Universe (in the form of a new sun, new planetary systems, or a new class of sentient beings), gestation alone can take *millions of years.* Then there is the actual birthing process, spanning millennia.

Barbara intuits that we are now coming to the end of that process, and are preparing to join the cosmic family as a newly emergent species of sentient beings. She describes what's going on with us now in these terms: "Our planet is a finite system. It is natural that our intelligent species has reached a limit of growth, just as we reached a limit of our own growth in the womb of our mother. It is natural that we've run out of nonrenewable resources. It is natural that many of us are waking up and beginning to see that these problems are actually evolutionary drivers, moving us toward invention and innovation in every field."

Hold It. Stop. Run Past That Again . . .

That may be the single most powerful thought I've heard in a very long time.

Let's look at it again.

The idea that what many people are calling "problems" are really *evolutionary drivers,* moving us toward invention and innovation in every field, is a mind-set that can not only inspire hope, but could actually *generate many of the innovations* that will pave the way to a wonderful future.

Now you may think that this is pie-in-the-sky philosophizing, so let me give you an example of how this *actually works,* in real terms.

As I write these words, the world is dealing with the explosion of a deep-sea oil rig in the Gulf of Mexico. As we all know, millions upon millions of gallons of oil began spilling into the gulf on April 20, 2010; and the leak wasn't contained until many weeks later. Estimates on exactly how much oil flowed into the sea vary widely, and the event has been called the worst environmental disaster faced by the United States in its history.

No one would begin to make light of, or dismiss, the negative impact of that event. Yet in the first part of the summer of 2010, two positive developments also occurred:

*1. The event awakened the sleeping giant of a nation's government and its citizens to the real and true need for clean energy alternatives—*something that years and years of talking could not do.

U.S. President Barack Obama said in the first televised statement of his Presidency from the Oval Office:

> For decades, we have known the days of cheap and easily accessible oil were numbered. For decades, we've talked and talked about the need to end America's century-long addiction to fossil fuels. And for decades, we have failed to act with the sense of urgency that this challenge requires. . . . The consequences of our inaction are now in plain sight. . . .
>
> We cannot consign our children to this future. The tragedy unfolding on our coast is the most painful and powerful reminder yet that the time to embrace a clean energy future is now. Now is the moment for this generation to embark on a national mission to unleash America's innovation and seize control of our own destiny.

There were signs that America's citizens, and even some of its powerful politicians, were beginning to see the light—and were prepared to embrace important changes in our energy policy.

2. The event awakened the innovative impulse of problem solvers not only in America, but around the world . . . including those at a high-technology textile-effects company based in Switzerland called HeiQ Materials, which announced in June the creation of a product, developed with the TWE Group in Germany, dubbed "Oilguard," that selectively absorbs oil while repelling water at the same time.

It is a fabric specially designed out of a nonwoven kind of fleece and treated with a chemical compound. It comes in sheets up to six yards wide and hundreds of yards long, which can be unfolded on shorelines and beaches in a matter of minutes to protect them from oil pollution. Once the material absorbs the oil, it can be easily rolled up and disposed of in an incineration plant, the company said. The company called it a powerful tool for protecting and cleaning up oil-strewn beaches in the Gulf of Mexico.

HeiQ representatives explained how the vast impact of the oil spill was *the "driving force" behind the development of this cutting-edge technology.*

Real-Time, On-the-Ground Help

Barbara Marx Hubbard believes that those who connect with each other and collaborate are helping in real time, on the ground, to give birth to that more co-creative, universal humanity of which she so often speaks.

"Enough of us are connecting in consciousness and creativity right now to realize that we are literally one planetary system, being born into a universe of untold dimensions and trillions of other planetary systems," she says.

And so we see that while this story is about Barbara's past, it is about everyone's future. It is about the next step in the process of our evolution. It is about where you and I and our children and our children's children are going.

That makes it, as I said before, not your ordinary biography. Remember that word I used earlier? What you're reading here is a *uniography.*

I made up that word. I use it to mean "the life story of an individual that turns out to be the life story of the Unified Whole, with a prediction of things to come arising out of things that have passed—because past, present, and future are a Unified Whole as well."

An Out-of-Place Author's Note

In line with that, I'm going to do something unusual here. I'm going to tell Barbara's story *backward* (more or less—although

39

there will be just a bit of "jumping around" on the time curve here and there), beginning with the already-experienced description of an envisioned future, and ending with a narrative of Barbara's distant past.

(Ordinarily I'd explain this in a Preface or an "Author's Note," but some people seldom read those, preferring to dive right into the main part of the book, so I'm going to explain myself here, *where I know all of you will read it!*)

I've chosen this "backward" approach because I believe that, as in the lives of all of us, there is much to be learned from hindsight. Looking backward, *after* events have occurred, makes this book feel more like real life to me. We all do this in our own lives, after all. We experience our Today, and all the events therein, and then we say, "Now how did that *happen?*" and we start looking at our Yesterdays, most recent to more distant, in that order.

It's a mystery, really. I see all of life as a mystery waiting to be solved, and so this is a *Mystery Story.* Like many good mystery stories, we're going to play detective here, moving backward from the scene before us and discovering, one by one, the elements and events that brought it about—revealing clearly the interplay between Cause and Effect, the role of Synchronicity, and the power of Prior Intention.

When you already know what's going to happen (because you have been given the end of the story first), it's easier to see *how* and *why* and *when it began* to happen. And seeing this in someone else's life may open the door for you to more clearly see this in your own. Individual occurrences are then seen as much larger happenings. Not as small events on this day or that, but as one Very Large Event taking place across a span of many months, or even years.

Viewed on this stretched canvas, the relationship between so many of life's moments becomes strikingly apparent. And that allows us to hold *this* moment, Right Here, Right Now, in a whole new way, appreciating it on an entirely different level.

A biography thus becomes instructive. It becomes, indeed, a *uniography*—the story of all of us.

Now, there could be some of you who may not particularly care for unraveling mysteries. You'd rather read a life story from beginning to end, as is traditionally done. So I've made it easy for you to do so, if you want to.

By presenting Barbara's story in Numbered Episodes, anyone not wanting to read it "in reverse" may simply jump to the closing pages and read the book *from back to front!* Just follow along from Episode 1 to Episode 25! (The timeline at the beginning of the book should come in handy.)

But I'd like to make this special Author's Request, please, regardless of how you approach the material:

Please don't try to keep track of all the names and relationships of all the people moving in and out of this story, or the precise sequencing of events. Attempting to do so will only engage your Mind in needless concentration on details—and that will divert you from the main point.

The point of the story here is that life is constantly conspiring to move forward our Soul's agenda; to answer our inner calling. The purpose of the narrative is not to get caught up in trying to follow intricate plotlines or specific facts, but to provide real-world evidence of *how life works*—and that it works the same way with all of us.

So now, and with that caveat, let's get back to the story itself.

EPISODE #24: THE BOOK, JANUARY 2010—
Two Years Before Day One . . .

Barbara Marx Hubbard is at my home in Ashland, Oregon. She has come here to be interviewed by me for this book. She's up ahead of the sun, cozy in our guest room, writing in longhand in a large black artist's journal.

She faces a slew of phone calls that need to be made before noon and, after that, a three-hour videotaping session at a small television studio a few blocks away. In between, she'll squeeze in a bit of breakfast.

This is how it goes with Barbara all the time. Things to do, things to do, *always* things to do—and nothing that is ever boring.

At present, she is doing her morning journaling. She is now on Volume 171. She made her first entry in Volume 1 at the age of 18, in 1947.

She was at Bryn Mawr College then, seeking the meaning of her life, and of human existence. In the years since, she has recorded every event and insight that has come to her. Her journaling has always been more than simple diary keeping. She describes situations just as anyone else would do in a diary, yes, but she also uses her journaling as a *process*. She learned to do that long ago. She asks for guidance, listens with a poised mind, writes the information down, and then tests out ideas that come to her.

The result is that her journals are more than just records. They have presaged and kept track of a "mystery story"—the story of not only her own, but *humanity's*, birthing as a new human—long before Barbara knew she was living it herself. In this mystery, she has been both the detective and the subject of her own sleuthing.

As we shall see while the mystery story unfolds—and as her journals, read in retrospect, now clearly reveal—she was being guided in her "mission" before it seemed obvious this was actually happening. And these days, she is beginning to act out what had been prophetically recorded in those old notebooks.

And so it is that January 2010 finds Barbara fervently going about the business of creating what many might call The Event of the Century. She and a few of her friends.

For Barbara, it's the culmination of a life's work, a life's vision, a life mission. It's the final expression of what she has often called "my vocation."

Where You Come In

We all have a "vocation," but some of us may not know how to activate it. One can feel the urge to bring beauty and goodness into the world (we all do), yet be at a loss as to how to make that happen.

Your Mission ("should you choose to accept it") may have already been made clear to you through a deep and undeniable feeling, as an intuitive knowing, through an expansive awareness, or as an unquenchable desire. Barbara often calls this experience "supra-sex."

"We've all heard about sex, but very few of us have heard about supra-sex," Barbara likes to say.

It's just after 9 A.M. and my wife, Em, and I have managed to coax Barbara upstairs into the kitchen with coffee, toast, and scrambled eggs. Reluctantly, she has left her morning journaling. It's difficult to stop that kind of writing when you know you've made the "connection." Still, one has to eat.

I'm smiling as I stand at the other end of the kitchen counter. "Okay, you've caught my attention. What's 'supra-sex'?"

"In sex, we join our genes to have a baby. In supra-sex, we join our *genius* to give birth to our greater selves and our work in the world."

She takes a sip of her coffee.

"It starts when you feel within you a frustration, or what I call a 'vocational arousal.' Your life purpose kicks up and hits you. Just as in puberty, you suddenly have to do something more, and you don't know how. What you have to do is *find your teammates* and *join together to co-create* in such a way that your life purpose gets manifested."

"Ah." I find myself nodding, as if I knew this all along.

"Nature put joy into sex, and guess what . . . She is putting joy into supra-sex. We follow the same compass, the compass of joy. With this compass we find each other. We are motivated not by what we want to get, but by what we want to *give*. We join to co-create."

I find Barbara's use of metaphor here to be stunning. And she doesn't stop there.

"This shift from maximum procreation to co-creation is natural, it's exciting, it's the greatest gift we are given. Love and supra-sex! The world won't be evolved through fear and guilt alone. It will also be evolved through love and creativity."

"So this is what the 2012 Day One event is all about," I surmise.

"Yes," Barbara confirms. "And that's what the Synergy Engine is designed for. It is to come online as part of that event on December 22, 2012; and its purpose will be to help people find their teammates, to help us all co-create in a synergistic way."

It All Starts with a Declaration

Yet finding one's teammates is not the first step in one's "vocation activation," as this look at Barbara's life will reveal. First, you must speak out about your calling. You must tell others—or your "teammates" *won't even know who they are.*

What I observe after talking extensively with Barbara is that one of the most powerful things she has done to *activate* her calling has been to *declare* it. This takes courage. It requires a willingness to be labeled a dreamer (maybe even an eccentric) and the strength to ignore being marginalized or patronized. And it takes the courage to shift the course of your life if you see that where you are going is not where you want to be.

(I love the quote from Douglas Engelbart, a Silicon Valley legend who is in his eighth decade, on this experience: "Someone once called me 'just a dreamer.' That offended me, the 'just' part; being a dreamer is hard work. It really gets hard when you start believing your dreams.")

Does that eliminate most of us? I don't think so. I believe that courage and willingness are qualities found in everyone. And once the Synergy Engine is online, believing in one's dreams will be natural—and actually *facilitated*. Yet we will still have to be willing and prepared to call them forth.

Barbara seems pensive now.

"Everything all right?" I inquire.

"Oh, yes," she replies lightly, and I watch her come back to the present moment. "I was just thinking . . ."

"Care to share?"

"Yes, thank you. I do, actually," she begins, and then turns to me, sitting on a stool next to her. "I've always been aware that I had a 'mission,' you know."

"Really? Always?"

"Well, from my very earliest years, yes."

I reach for a pen and tablet. I want to catch this.

"And just what is your mission?"

"For the last 50 years it has been: 'Go tell the story of our birth. Help catalyze a planetary birth experience for humanity.'"

She says it simply, not seeming to notice how grandiose it might sound to others.

(Now you see, that is where the courage comes in. You've got to say what's true for you, no matter how others might take it. For sure, you'll want to find a way to state things in such a way that others can "hear you"—but in the end, you must be brave enough to avoid retreating just when you start to look a bit like Don Quixote.)

"You know, when you say that," I observe, "you sound as if someone has *given* you that mission."

She smiles. "Someone has, but it is only very recently that I've had a clue as to the *source* of this guidance." Then a twinkle blesses her eye. "I guess I don't have to tell *you* about that."

"No," I chuckle, "you don't." I glance at a copy of *Conversations with God* on the kitchen counter.

The "Assignment" Givers

I, too, have had this idea that I was given an "assignment." My task, my invitation, was to change the world's mind about God. (That's all!) Just change the world's mind about Who and What God is, about what God wants, and about the reason and purpose of human life. I was to gather information about this directly from Divine Intelligence, write down the conversations I was having with It, then have them typed up and sent to a publisher. It was made clear to me that this is all I needed to do. Everything else would be taken care of.

It was.

I could have never imagined that seven and a half million people would read the books that grew of out that experience, or that those books would be published in 37 languages and produce seven *New York Times* bestsellers. But then, this is how the process works.

Barbara couldn't have imagined where her life would lead her either. Could she have ever dreamed that she would have her name placed in nomination for Vice President of the United States at the national convention of one of its two major political parties? No. Could she have conjured the image of herself leading several U.S. delegations to the Soviet Union to help close the cultural/political gap between those two nations? No.

And most of all, could she possibly have known that to her, and a critical mass of others on the planet, would fall the task of bringing humanity the news of its most monumental moment—the moment of its own birthing into the Universal Community of Self-Realized Beings?

Uh . . . no.

Not at first. Eventually, yes. Eventually, Barbara would become very clear that this was her calling. But could she have imagined that early on? No. Not in such specific terms. She knew—oh boy, did she ever know!—even as a child, that there was something important that she was supposed to do, but in those days she couldn't figure out what it was.

And so it is with most of us. Each of us must move through the revealing and the playing out of our "mission" step-by-step. That takes faith in the process. And that is why Barbara's story is important. It offers us inspiration, and it gives us a basis for having that faith.

"So this is a process of evolution," I venture between bites of toast.

"Not so much evolution as *involution*," Barbara explains. "It is the Spirit that has been descending into Matter, Life, Animal Life, Humans, and now Universal Humans—embodying itself and lifting up evolving humans.

"In my case, that Spirit is saying: 'Remember Me into reality. You have come from where I have come from. You have incarnated in this lifetime to serve as a guide through the transition.'"

"Humanity's transition," I offer, my eggs growing cold.

"Yes," Barbara confirms.

Her cell phone rings, and now her breakfast is going to grow cold, too. It doesn't matter. She's used to it. And on this functional level (getting food into her body, finding a place to sleep, and so forth), she is easy to please. Whatever is going on is what works. "Excuse me," she says, looking at the caller ID. "I've got to take this."

Barbara leaves the kitchen and strolls into the living room, the cell phone to her ear, her mind already switched to a new track. I'm left to muse over what she's just said.

Is it possible that I actually had a conversation with God? I don't doubt it for a moment. I never would have written nine books of dialogue if I hadn't experienced it to be exactly that. So I understand if Barbara feels that she has communicated with Someone Outside Herself—who also resides *within*. I'm wondering not whether such a thing happened, but just how she experienced it.

She has come back to the room now, and I reengage our conversation. "God said to me that God is talking with all of us, with every single human being, all the time."

Explaining Future You

"I'm sure that's true." Barbara nods. "And Divinity comes in many forms." Then she tells me that her "assignment" came to her from what she is just now beginning to experience as a universal being. "A Universal Being is a partner 'postbirth,'" she explains, "but not necessarily someone else."

"Postbirth?"

"A being who has been through its own planetary birth on its own planet and is now more mature than we are—yet related by having been born from the same cosmos, from its Earth womb, and who made it through its own crisis of birth and therefore had the experience needed by us now. This being is not here to do it for us—the birth, I mean—but to offer awareness, as parents and family do to a newborn infant."

"But you said it wasn't necessarily someone else."

"That's right. This being is not someone apart and separate from us. This being is *our very Self* . . . in the future, fully realized."

I let that stay there for a while. I want to think about that.

Barbara honors my silence. Then, after a good, quiet interlude . . .

"I feel I've been guided by such a being, by my Higher Self, since 1945. But I didn't realize it until after our own space program got under way in the '60s, and I didn't have an *experiential* reference for it until a morning in 2002 in Montecito, California. . . .

"It was when I saw the astronauts land on the moon that I realized that we are becoming extraterrestrials ourselves, and I sensed that my guidance was so specific around my role as a storyteller of the planetary birth experience that it may well have come from another source, a being who has already been 'born' as a Universal Being."

I ask, "How did you feel about this thought? Did you fear that you were spinning out, losing touch with reality, dancing with wild ideas?"

"Not at all." Barbara laughs. "I actually thought, *Why not?* And now, of course, after my Montecito experience, it seems perfectly normal and perfectly logical to me. It's probably true that many of us are receiving very specific guidance from our 'future selves' and 'higher selves' about our new role in the evolution of our world. In fact, all of us are—it's just that not everyone is noticing it, or paying attention to it."

I certainly can't argue with *that*. Yet I have never heard Barbara talk about such things within the context of her own experiences. Not in such specific terms.

"That explains a lot about all that has been happening in your life for the past 60 years," I observe.

"Yes, it does," she acknowledges.

A Catalyst, Not an Exemplar

"So . . . are you then a role model for this new human that is about to be birthed?"

I become aware by her actions that Barbara wants to be very clear now. She has put down her lukewarm coffee and pushes it away from her just a bit, as if to say, *Okay, done with that. Now this is all I want to focus on—what I'm going to say right now.*

You can tell when a person has moved into that let's-get-clear-about-this space. It is where Barbara is, and I listen closely.

"I've come here to act not as an exemplar," she says quietly, "but as a catalyst." (I come to find out later that she has answered this question before.)

"A catalyst for . . . ?"

"For so many others who are right at the threshold of their own emergence."

"Emergence into what?"

Again, Barbara pauses. And now she speaks very slowly and deliberately.

"We used to project all these new capacities onto our gods. But since we ourselves are learning to extend our intelligence through more rapid and more extensive communication, to alter our bodies, to live in space, and even build new worlds in space . . . I realized that something stunning is occurring. We've projected our own potential onto our gods, and we are now bringing that potential home as our own. We are becoming what we used to call gods."

"Why now?" I want to know. "Why not last year, last decade, or last century? Why is this happening during these days?"

"Because it is time. Because Science and Technology have given us new powers, greater than humans have ever had before. Now we can truly call ourselves very young Universal Humans. Earth is like a kindergarten for 'godlings'—all of us who are ready and willing! But we have to learn ethical, conscious evolution quickly. That means to love each other, and nature, as ourselves. If we don't do this, we will self-destruct. *That* is the real drama."

"And you see yourself as a catalyst for all this."

"Yes . . . me and many others."

"Still, you say that you're not different from anyone else."

"I'm not," she says, smiling. She plays with the spoon that she'd set on the saucer next to the coffee cup. She's buying time. There's something more she wants to say, and she wants to get this right, too.

"It is true," she begins slowly, "that I've had to work to raise myself to a certain level of what I would term 'harmonics' in order to be sensitized enough to 'connect' in this way."

"You mean to connect with this Universal Being, with this Higher Self?"

"Yes. And also to connect in this way with you . . . and with everyone else."

I understand this. When one is at that level of "harmonics," I've learned, certain things happen, certain things start falling into place; life becomes vastly different. *We* may be no different from others, but our *lives* start to look different. We get asked to run for Vice President. We get asked to go to Russia to promote world harmony. We get asked to midwife humanity in its birthing, to help an entire species reinvent itself. We become . . . the Mother of Invention. And we become a Future Human.

That would be a fitting way to describe Barbara Marx Hubbard.

🌾 🌾 🌾

What We All Want to Know

As we reflect on the times just described, and look more closely at Barbara's experience to see what we all might benefit from,
we are reminded that . . .

> **. . . there are two things that call to the human
> heart and soul, that pull on us, tug at us. We are
> concerned with who we are and why we are here.
> We want to know about our Identity and our Calling.**

Each of us has a vocation, and when we are "vocationally
aroused," as Barbara would put it, our opportunity and invitation
from life is not to deny that, but to muster the courage to step
into that fully—first by boldly declaring our calling and then by
bravely activating it.

Yet let us explore a thought about that. If we seem unable to
"activate our calling" in the way we think or imagine we are *supposed* to, or in the way we most *desire,* does that mean we have
"failed"?

This is a question that all people must face, for nearly every
person on Earth has imagined that he or she has failed at one

thing or another. This is a false thought. Nothing we've ever thought, said, or done has produced anything but *forward movement.* It is impossible for evolution to progress in any other direction. There is only *forward,* one thing building upon another . . . each event, each circumstance, each situation a gift. Each a part of a sacred process.

There is also the awareness that we are not here to produce a particular expression in our outer environment in any event, but rather, an experience in our inner world. And the irony is that when we produce that experience in our inner world, our outer environment changes in wondrous ways automatically, as a natural consequence of our own evolution.

And when we do this as a *group*—that is, as an entire *species*— we actually re-create ourselves anew. It is, truly, a birthing on a planetary scale.

To achieve this, we must ban the thought of "failure" forever. We must be clear that *however* things have turned out, we have not failed—rather, we have played our important role in the outpicturing and evolving of Self and Tomorrow. One thing leads to another, inexorably, and everything benefits that process and *produces* it.

We will explore this phenomenon deeply in the pages ahead, through the telling of more and more of Barbara's story.

Enjoy.

ℒ ℒ ℒ

9.

EPISODE #23: THE CALL THAT IGNITES DAY ONE, NOVEMBER 16, 2009—Two Months Before the Ashland Interview That Began the Process of Creating the Book . . .

What a night it has been! Barbara is attending a gala event in Los Angeles focusing on using the entertainment media to create a better world. There are 500 people in the room, including some Hollywood luminaries and behind-the-scenes movers and shakers.

Barbara had no idea just how much this night would mean to her when a friend, Claudia Welss, invited her. Only after things rolled out the way they did could she see its significance.

When she first arrived, she thought, *What am I doing here?* There were multimedia screens set up, and young people everywhere. Clearly this was about contemporary, edgy media; and Barbara, at 79, couldn't help feeling a little out of place.

Then a new acquaintance from within that group of young media professionals, a woman named Kate McCallum, approaches her. "I'm so glad you're here!" she beams.

"Well, thank you," Barbara replies. "But I'm curious. Why?"

"You inspired me ten years ago, and this whole event was in many ways inspired by you."

Before Barbara can respond, she sees an old friend, Jerome Glenn, head of The Millennium Project for the U.N., heading toward her. She knows that he is the evening's keynote speaker. Although they hadn't seen each other in some time, Jerry had worked with Barbara in years past in some very important ways; and now, when he spots her in the room before the program begins, he moves immediately to her and they exchange a big hug.

"How perfect that you're here," he remarks, smiling. Now that's the *second* time Barbara has heard that! Again, she's a bit taken aback.

Once the program begins, even more such remarks and compliments pour from the panel onstage. Some of its members single Barbara out as the "mother of transformational entertainment" because she had produced and appeared in The Theater for the Future, a live multimedia show in Los Angeles 30 years earlier; and had broadcast many conferences about humanity's next evolutionary step on whatever media was available.

Now, Jerry Glenn, during his keynote speech, is tossing verbal bouquets Barbara's way, noting in glowing terms that she was one of the earliest exponents of the use of global media to change the planet and alter the way humanity experiences itself.

"I'm so glad to give thanks to Barbara," he is saying, "who has helped me and others in understanding a new worldview and using the media on its behalf."

Barbara never hears the compliment.

As it is being delivered, *she* is being delivered, in an ambulance, to a nearby hospital.

A Moment Before . . .

Sitting in the audience, Barbara suddenly feels a sharp stabbing pain deep in her stomach. She'd gone through this before, six years earlier. But she had surgery for that—it was a ruptured appendix—so what could *this* be?

Thinking it's just a bad cramp, she tries to ignore it. No dice. The pain hits again. Now she knows something is wrong. Terribly wrong.

Slowly rising from her seat, she slips out of the auditorium, hobbling to the ladies' room, where she is brought to tears by the pain; and then, with a deep cleansing breath, tries to power through it. That seems to work, as the pain subsides.

Starting back for her seat, she gets as far as the center of the lobby before a third jolt of pain nearly brings her to the floor. She wobbles to a nearby bench and folds over.

A volunteer sees her and rushes over.

"Are you okay? Do you want to go to the hospital?"

Still hoping that whatever it is will pass, Barbara shakes her head. But she can barely speak, and then she winces again. The color in her face suddenly doesn't look so good. The volunteer runs off.

A friend happens by—Rev. Michael Beckwith, a minister widely known for, among other things, his inspiring appearance in the movie *The Secret*. Others show up, too, including the folks with whom Barbara is attending the event. Wondering why she has been gone for so long, they'd left the auditorium to check on her. They move quickly to her side.

Everyone immediately sees that Barbara is in genuine distress. Holding her hand, Michael asks the same question the volunteer asked.

"Do you want to go to the hospital?"

Again, she declines, but it's too late. An ambulance has already arrived, and paramedics are scrambling around the lobby, led by the volunteer—who apparently thought Barbara definitely needed medical help.

It's a good thing. At the hospital, a doctor tells Barbara: "I think you have a blocked colon."

My God . . . first a ruptured appendix, now a blocked colon. Hmm, not exactly a stomach cramp, Barbara muses. Her eyes dart around the emergency room, capturing a scene that is looking increasingly surreal. "I thought I was in a sitcom," she would say later. "The doctor looked like someone on a stage set. He said they wanted to see if the colon would 'unblock' naturally. If not, I would have to have surgery."

Barbara is admitted to intensive care. It is November 16. She will be in the hospital until the second day of December.

The Blessing of Time to Think

Barbara spends the first week under observation, connected to tubes everywhere. She is intaking through veins and outflowing through catheters. Finally, there's news: It had nothing to do with her colon. It was all about the small upper intestine. More critically, the situation is not clearing up. Surgery will be necessary.

On November 23, the operation proceeds. It is to remove lesions and a small section of her intestine, and it goes off without a hitch. Still, this is not something you hop out of bed and walk away from. Especially not at 80, which Barbara will be in a few weeks. So Good Samaritan Hospital remains her home for nine more days.

During her first days there, the friends with whom she had gone to the gala stop by for a visit and tell her about all of the wonderful words of praise she'd missed, and the thanks that had been sent her way that night. Her eyes brighten. She wasn't "out of place" in that room full of Hollywood writers and producers and other media professionals—young as most of them were—after all. She was *one of them.*

Normally a person of endless motion and vigorous activity, the downtime allows Barbara—forces her, actually—to do nothing but think. And so, she spends two solid weeks asking herself: *How can I mobilize this moment? There's a _reason_ I was drawn to Los Angeles for this unlikely event, there's a _reason_ all these people were saying these things to me, and there's a _reason_ why I've been put in a position in which I can do nothing but contemplate this.*

As it happens, the reason is about to reveal itself—and the "mother of transformational entertainment" was simply being placed in a state of mind where she could fully embrace and totally accept what was to occur next. . . .

Creation of the Day One Event Begins

Five days following her operation, the healing is steady but slow. Then, in a sure sign that things are better, people one day start piling into her room—doctors, nurses, and technicians. They've come to remove all the tubes. She's "unhooked" at last.

Minutes later her cell phone rings. She answers.

"Hello?"

"Hello, Barbara."

The man on the other end introduces himself, and all Barbara can do is laugh.

"Oh, no! What an appropriate time for you to call! I was just the bionic woman," she remarks, laughing, "but now I'm back to normal."

It's a call she's been expecting, from someone she'd met 30 years earlier, but she certainly hadn't been expecting to take it here. On the other hand, he knew she was in the hospital, and that's why he called just then. He wanted to check on her. She explains what has been happening, and what has *just* happened—that they had just taken the tubes out—and the two chuckle. Then . . .

"But you're okay, yes?"

"Oh yes, quite okay, thank you. It's been an interesting experience, and I've been brought back to remembering a few things—a few very important things—and I'm *very* okay."

"I'm so glad. And I'm sorry if I got you at an awkward moment. I was just wanting to make contact and send you my wishes for your fast recovery."

"No, no, don't apologize. For goodness' sake, don't apologize. I'm glad to hear your voice."

The two make quick arrangements to talk more when she's back at home. "It shouldn't be more than a few days," she assures him.

They say good-bye, but there will be many more conversations between these two.

Many more . . .

10.

EPISODE #22: COLLABORATORS ARE FOUND, APRIL 2009—
Seven Months Before the Call That Ignites Day One . . .

It may seem like there's no connection between the event now to be described and the episode just related—the phone call in the hospital room—but it's all part of a mosaic. And the two men involved in these episodes are soon to meet.

It is a fairly normal day weatherwise in Boulder, Colorado. The temperature on this month's first Friday reaches 58 degrees by noon, and while that couldn't compete with the record April highs back in '91 (it had reached 82 degrees on the same day that year), most folks in this Rocky Mountain community are perfectly happy.

Barbara, who is here for a special recording project with a man named Darrell Laham, might have had a fleeting, wistful thought of her home in Santa Barbara, where it would normally be much warmer. But, irony of ironies, on this day, California is in the midst of a cool wave, and it is exactly the same temperature there.

The recording that Barbara is taking part in is for *The Cosmic Family Reunion,* a dramatic piece written by her years earlier, which first came to the attention of Darrell Laham eight months prior to this meeting. It had such an impact on him that he asked if he might get her to produce an audio track of it with him. And *now* they are doing just that.

It is during a break in the session that Barbara and Darrell find themselves chatting about the possibility of obtaining funding to bring into creation a decades-long dream of hers that is prominently mentioned at the climax of the dramatic reading. She calls it a "Peace Room."

"It would be like the War Room that we know the government now has, which maps every enemy and how to defeat them," she explains. "In the Peace Room, however, we would look for breakthroughs and innovations that are working.

"It would be able to monitor every trouble spot on Earth—but this would be a different kind of monitoring. In the Peace Room, we would compile every good idea, every working solution that has been put in place to address a problem anywhere, so that people and communities facing the same situation could be instantly connected with those innovations, which could be replicated or adapted quickly and easily, all around the world."

"Ingenious—and so painfully obvious," Darrell says, shaking his head. "Pay attention to what *is* working rather than to what is *not* working."

"Exactly," Barbara nods.

"*That* is what can create peace. I see why you call it the Peace Room—it's peace through co-creation and collaboration."

"Yes. We know that even now, wonderful ideas are being applied, and terrific solutions are being discovered all over the planet. We just don't *know* about them. There is genius everywhere, from major cities to small towns and tiny villages . . . and all the places in between.

"All we need is the technology to scan for, map, connect, communicate, and compare solutions 'here' with problems 'there.' And . . . ," Barbara hints tantalizingly, "I think we may have found the funding."

Darrell practically jumps out of his chair.

"I have that technology!" he blurts out. "I know exactly how to *do* that!"

The "Cast" Gets Larger

Barbara then tells Darrell about the next step for the Peace Room: to expand its intent to produce not only global collaboration, but global coherence. This prompts an excited call by the two of them to yet another new "player" on the stage—a one-time student, now friend of Barbara's, named Claudia Welss, who added the "coherence" idea to the mix a few months previously.

Inspired by Barbara's concept of social synergy, in 2006 Claudia had created the NextNow Collaboratory, a nonprofit collaboration lab to match needs with resources for social-benefit projects. By May 2008, she was participating in an intensive led by Barbara called "Conscious Evolution and Social Synergy: Toward an Evolutionary Politics" at a church in Oakland, California.

Claudia submitted a paper based on the intensive and informed by her work with the Global Coherence Initiative called "Subtle Realms of Social Synergy." In it, she identified what she believed was "something missing" in the design of the Wheel of Co-Creation: intentionally constructing a "coherent energetic architecture" that would invite deep and persistent synergy and thereby accelerate synergistic convergence—and our conscious evolution.

"If we need to design the actual processes for social synergy, then do we not also need to consciously design—as in, fashion the form and structure of—the field that will energize these processes?" Claudia asked. "Without our conscious design, it is our unconscious that will inform its structure. Attention to this energetic architecture is as important as attention to the social architecture in designing for social synergy."

Barbara was elated. Not only had she been given a wonderful additional insight, but she had also found a brilliant new collaborator.

And so, Barbara and Darrell call her now to ask for her input in how to best position the Peace Room as a powerful "enabler of our planetary birth experience." This conversation will help define the Synergy Engine that will be created for the Day One event in 2012 as a true synergy platform.

In addition to the paper she had written, Claudia had been discussing with Barbara at length how she believed energetic coherence was critical to creating the conditions for full and authentic synergistic convergence to occur.

"Buckminster Fuller once defined synergy as 'synthesis + energy,'" Claudia had offered in one of those exchanges. "This definition implies that the quality of personal energy we apply in creating synergy *matters*. Coherent energy is persistent and creates effect; incoherent energy cancels itself out. If the Synergy Engine could help reflect the level of coherence of the social body and encourage cultivating *coherence as a social function,* it would result in a higher quality of synergy."

"And what about creating a kind of receptivity, harmony, openness, and attraction for whatever is beyond us—something that is sufficient enough to invite contact?" Barbara asked.

"Well, my guess is a planet vibrating at the frequency of coherence would make a great contribution toward creating those conditions. In a coherent system, information flows more freely; think about how *we* feel when we feel coherent as opposed to incoherent! In 'collective coherence,' information would flow more freely not just *within* the social body, but also *with* the greater intelligence in which it is embedded.

"In my mind's eye, a coherent Earth would be sufficiently bright (and sufficiently beautiful) to be noticed from space by any Intelligence that might be watching."

And so the three—Barbara, Darrell, and Claudia—begin moving the Peace Room idea to the next level of expression: a means of creating deeper synergy in the social body through coherence, with the added benefit of producing sufficient synergy on Earth in order to attract the interest of sources of higher intelligence elsewhere, demonstrating that humanity is, indeed, ready for "contact."

EPISODE #21: THE MILLION-DOLLAR QUESTION, APRIL 2009—
The Day Before the Collaborators Are Found . . .

Bundled in a robe and slippers, Barbara scrambles in search of her chiming cell phone. In one of life's little triumphs, she finds it before it stops ringing.

"Hello?"

"Barbara, dear, this is Suzanne Mendelssohn."

Suzanne is a "telephone friend." She and Barbara have never met in person, but they have had important conversations by phone over the previous six years, with Suzanne acting as a healer for Barbara, and most recently involving Barbara's son, Wade.

"Yes, Suzanne, how are you?"

"I'm fine, thank you. Barbara, I have a question to ask you."

"Okay . . ."

"If you had a million dollars at your disposal, what would you do to help humanity make positive contact with extraterrestrials?"

That is not the kind of question one would anticipate in an unexpected telephone call first thing in the morning. Barbara had never seen an extraterrestrial, nor had she given much thought to the idea of contacting one. Yet she had imagined the experience of a planetary birth, a collective awakening, a "planetary smile," that would enable us to open our collective eyes and see the light together. . . .

Barbara's answer flies out of her mouth as if she'd been waiting to be asked that for 25 years: "I would create a 'Welcoming Committee' made up of scientifically based, spiritually sensitive people in every sector of the Wheel of Co-Creation. They would be a point of contact to *welcome humanity to itself* as a whole, and to welcome higher beings to communicate with us in that moment of mass resonance and awakening. They would help us lift our own vibrations high enough to receive whatever lies beyond. Oh, and we would need to have the Peace Room online."

"That's what I thought you'd say." Suzanne's voice is more animated now. "Barbara, I've come across a man who is willing to provide funding to Edgar Mitchell to the tune of $1 billion; and if this goes through, I would get 10 percent for having raised it for him. From that percentage, we'd have the funds that you need to put together the Welcoming Committee and Peace Room."

An Old Acquaintance Rejoins the Cast

William Shakespeare said it, and it couldn't have been put better:

All the world's a stage,
And all the men and women merely players.
They have their exits and their entrances,
And one man in his time plays many parts . . .

Edgar Mitchell is a longtime acquaintance of Barbara's. He is, of course, the world-famous former American astronaut—the sixth person to walk on the moon. As might be expected, that event changed his life . . . but in an unexpected way. At least, unexpected by those who didn't know him well.

A man who began his career very much as a traditionalist, he went public after his moon walk as very much a *non*traditionalist. (He earned a bachelor of science degree in industrial management from Carnegie Institute of Technology in 1952 and the following year joined the U.S. Navy, where he later qualified as a research pilot, earned a master's degree in aeronautical engineering, and obtained a doctorate in aeronautics and astronautics from MIT.)

Mitchell raised eyebrows when he revealed that on his way to the moon, during the *Apollo 14* flight on which he was the lunar-module pilot, he had conducted private ESP experiments with some friends back on Earth.

He then surprised even more people when, a few months following his retirement from the Navy in 1972, he formed the nonprofit Institute of Noetic Sciences, which he said would sponsor and conduct scientific research into the nature of consciousness, psychic events, and the connection between mind and matter. He felt that what is needed is verifiable scientific exploration of these vital questions.

Moreover, the former astronaut went on record stating that he's convinced we have been (and are continuing to be) visited by beings from far beyond our own solar system. He believes that some governments of the world are hiding this fact, and that evidence of these visitations is virtually irrefutable.

When Barbara hears of the Edgar Mitchell connection, her heart jumps. "Is this real?" she asks.

"I think so," her friend replies. "Yes, I think so."

"Because if it is, I would need much more than that to build the Peace Room!"

Suzanne laughs. Barbara's ideas never get smaller, just larger. That's the only direction her mind moves in—always and only into The Bigger.

"Yes, dear," Suzanne allows, "but we have to start somewhere . . ."

"I suppose." Barbara joins in the chuckle. "But I really have to know if this is real. Who is this person with a billion dollars?"

"He's a man you met 30 years ago. . . ."

🌿 🌿 🌿

REFLECTIONS & EXPLORATIONS

The Universe Has a Reason for Everything

As we reflect on the times just described, and look more closely at Barbara's experience to see what we all might benefit from, we are reminded that . . .

> **. . . people weave in and out of our lives in ways that may seem random—but they never are.**

I'm going to invite you to remember what I said earlier: Please don't try to keep track of all the people and places moving in and out of this story, or the precise sequencing of events. Attempting to do so will only focus your Mind on details—and that will divert you from the overarching point. The point of the story is that life is constantly conspiring to move your Soul's agenda forward, to answer your inner calling.

Life is a far more organized production than most of us give it credit for. It's like a well-written movie. And, as in a movie, nobody and nothing appears on screen without purpose.

As we move through the moments of our lives and encounter the people we meet, all of this can be helpful to understand. For then, we may interact with those individuals in an entirely different way. At the very least, we'll let them see who we really are—and not be standoffish or distant. For all paths ultimately turn in on themselves, and nothing we do or say today is without impact on some tomorrow. I promise you.

There is a theory out there that suggests that we move through all of our lifetimes with the same relatively small number of souls. Indeed, this theory asserts that these are not different souls at all, but *one soul* divided into many parts.

The idea is that just as God divides itself into many parts (called "souls") so that Divinity might experience The Whole of itself, so too do individual souls divide *themselves* into parts—and for exactly the same reason.

If this is true, we are simply meeting our Selves over and over again in the form of the other parts of our Soul—who become some of the significant others of every lifetime. I find this a fascinating thought that has begun to color my response to people I'm meeting for the first time.

You never know when someone who is entering your life is really *returning* to your life to continue an Eternal Partnership. Perhaps that person is even ready to give you a million dollars to move your lifework to completion, or the million-dollar gift of deep friendship or true love.

Barbara's life also reminds us that . . .

> **. . . things happen the way they happen, *when*
> they happen, *where* they happen, for a reason—
> all of which is in perfect order, reflecting the
> perfection of the Universe and of Life itself.**

At one point, Barbara was wondering why she accepted the invitation to that Los Angeles event and what she was doing there with all those young people in the first place, and she was also wondering why in the world Life put her in the hospital that night. Before very long, however, she understood the reasoning for both experiences.

Her presence at the event raised the consciousness of the speakers regarding her contributions to the effort to use global media to help change the world—and in turn, because of the comments her presence inspired, she was reinspired to continue her work even more vigorously.

Every so often, all of us need such a boost, and Life will provide it for us just when we need it most—but we have to see it for what it is. Had she heard the praise of others while sitting in the room, Barbara could have been tempted to mentally wave them off with a graceful smile and a gracious thank-you, not thinking about them anymore. It's not as if she hadn't heard such glowing compliments before.

But Life wanted her to really *hear* these particular comments and consider them carefully; to look closely at what Life was telling her and ruminate on how she could best use the energy behind those remarks to move her life mission forward. The best way to do so? Get her to *stop everything,* if only briefly, and provide her with a chance to deeply reflect . . . at just the right moment in her life.

All of this would create a context for the call that was to come on her cell phone—and which she normally would have answered while in the midst of some important activity, but which she now received *while lying in the hospital* with nothing else to do but *think about the next step she would take* in her lifelong assignment *at the very moment* that the man who could provide the resources to make that next step possible *was on the other end of the line.*

My, my, my . . . what a tapestry, what a design! And so, we have to have faith. Faith in the process of Life itself, faith in what some of us choose to call "God," and faith in ourselves and the ability to embrace the Divine Design with gratitude—and play our Divine role *within* it.

When I speak about playing our role within a design, what I'm talking about is finding a way to walk in harmony with the events of the day, knowing that these occurrences—all of them, no matter what they are—are not meant to oppose you, but to compose you. That is, not to tear you apart, but to put you together.

So when what you label as "bad things" happen, *compose yourself.* Know that what is occurring is God, composing a poem. You are a work of art. The events of your life are the individual lines and stanzas. Not all will be completely understood until the poem is read to the end. But in the end, all will make perfect sense—and perfect beauty.

Through this remarkable interweaving, we're going to see that Life's most challenging moments *always* create opportunity.

"Always" means just that. It is true in every case. And while no one would *wish* for some kind of tragedy or emergency to occur in order to *produce* an opportunity, it can be useful to understand at a deep level how Life works. Knowing that there is a *benefit to every event* can help us find the strength to move through all the events of our lives with equanimity.

We will explore this truth deeply on the pages ahead, through the telling of more and more of Barbara's story.

Enjoy.

✻ ✻ ✻

11.

EPISODE #20: THE MAGICAL "ATTRACTOR," AUGUST 2008—
Eight Months Before the Million-Dollar Question . . .

Darrell Laham has found himself drawn to a most unlikely place—Hummingbird Ranch, on 500 acres of lush and breathtaking land nestled at the foot of the Sangre de Cristo Mountains in northern New Mexico at an altitude of 7,500 feet—to attend a participatory workshop on Evolutionary Leadership led by futurist and visionary Barbara Marx Hubbard.

The program includes a dramatic reading of Barbara's work *The Cosmic Family Reunion,* which was written in 1995. It is a myth in which a modern Eve asks to see the Lord God Yahweh face-to-face. He invites her to the Garden, where she confronts Him on what He has done to her (and all women as a consequence).

Lucifer is a character in the story, as might be expected, and in this participatory workshop, attendees were assigned to read the various parts as an opportunity to get in touch with archetypes that exist in each of us.

The story ends with a triumphant description of the vast celebration of a Planetary Birthday Party, in which the Peace Room is made available for everyone on Earth to use as a place to offer their gifts, as well as find solutions to the world's problems in the gifts of others. The idea is described as the key that opens human-kind to an alternative to Armageddon.

Darrell is transfixed as he listens at one point to Lucifer—representing the Separated Mind that is now in power—plaintively admit: "I don't even know what went wrong . . ."

Darrell begins to weep softly, and Barbara does not fail to notice.

"What does this mean to you?" she asks quietly.

And just as quietly, Darrell replies: "I saw for the first time a redeemed Lucifer inside myself. It's that part of me that went after power successfully. I could always feel a slight tension between love and power. I went with power . . . and I didn't even know what went wrong."

Darrell feels released by the story that Barbara has written, in which, later in the script, Eve forgives the Father for putting her in such a difficult position, and He is thereby redeemed.

During a break after the reading, Darrell tells Barbara that he feels a deep impulse to commit her work to a digital recording, and that he has an audio studio in his home in Boulder, Colorado, where he could do just that. He wants others to hear *The Cosmic Family Reunion*. He wants it saved for posterity. Would she be willing to join him in the project? Barbara thinks it's a splendid idea, and they agree to "one day do this."

They arrange the date months later, quite innocently, having no way of knowing that it would come within 24 hours of Barbara hearing about the possibility of a million-dollar grant that could turn the Peace Room (which is such a big part of the celebration scene of that very reading) into reality—something that Barbara has wanted to do for much of her adult life, and something that might, one day, even make her a bit more "famous." Not that fame was what she was after . . . but, you know, being a little better known can sometimes help you get things done.

EPISODE #19: DEATH GIVES NEW LIFE, AUGUST 2007— 12 Months Before the Magical "Attractor" . . .

Barbara Marx Hubbard hasn't yet managed to tell humanity, in any large way, about the story of its birth as a universal species, nor has she managed to make the Peace Room a reality. It exists only as an idea, as in the dramatic reading she'd written many years before; and since then in various proposals, abbreviated versions, and events that she has called "SYNCONS."

(First developed by Barbara and her life companion at the time, John Whiteside, in 1972, SYNCON is an acronym for "Synergistic Convergence"—meetings featuring the coming together of all vital elements of the social body to discover their functional relationships to each other and to the whole. You'll hear much more about this later, as we move backward in time through Barbara's life.)

Barbara is feeling frustrated that she still hasn't accomplished what she believes she came to the planet to do. She is never more aware of this fact than when her 46-year-old son, Wade, looks at her one day and says, quite unexpectedly, "Mom, why aren't you famous yet?"

The question, startling enough on its own, has double the impact because of the moment in which Wade poses it.

He is on his deathbed.

Cancer is killing him.

Because of this timing, Barbara hears this question—really *hears it*—and wonders if she'll ever get "on the radar" as The Storyteller. Will she ever bring a large swath of humanity (large enough to make a difference) the tale of its own birthing into the galactic community of highly evolved beings?

Wade had always encouraged her, always supported her in her work, and was always trying to figure out ways in which he could help. But now he was very weak, and not many days later, the cancer would take him. And so on this day, he can only ask about her. There was no longer going to be much more that he could do.

Unless . . .

"A very interesting thing has happened," Barbara will tell friends weeks later. "The night after Wade died, I received a deep intuitive message from him: *Contact Stanley Weiss. He'll help you build the Peace Room.* It was very specific and clear—and not something that I would have even thought of, or done, on my own."

Stanley Weiss had been Barbara's first beau, and Wade had heard the story many times. But she hadn't spoken to Stanley in 20 years, and Wade had never even met the man. Stanley had followed Barbara to Paris during her junior year of college abroad, but there she met Earl Hubbard, an artist with whom she fell in love and who was to become her husband—and Wade's father.

Seeing that clearly a match had been made, Stanley left Paris in despair and traveled to Mexico. While there, he became a student of the Mayan culture; founded a manganese mine; became very wealthy; and created an important Washington, D.C.–based organization called Business Executives for National Security. Stanley came to know generals and presidents throughout the world, especially in the Far East.

So why should Barbara suddenly contact him now, out of the blue?

"Wade's message was very clear," she explained, when talking with me about it for this book. "I couldn't ignore it. So that day I e-mailed, through his company, a man I hadn't seen in two decades. He gave me the courtesy of a call back, and we had a very nice conversation. But the key part about it was that as we spoke, my idea of the Peace Room came up—and our talk around that set something into motion that *reignited* in me the vision of that project, which we are now calling the Synergy Engine. And so, Wade's death gave me new life. His gift to me kept on coming . . ."

EPISODE #18: A CHANCE MEETING? JUNE 2007—
Two Months Before Death Gives New Life . . .

You see, the thing is that you never know—I mean, you just *never know*—what role someone is going to play in your life. All you *can* know is that there is *some* role, or the person wouldn't be anywhere near you. . . .

Barbara Marx Hubbard is a keynote speaker at a meeting of the Society for Scientific Exploration in East Lansing, Michigan. In the audience is a young man with long hair and rumpled clothes. He looks like a lonely postgrad student. He approaches Barbara after her talk, and as they chat, she finds herself intrigued by some of the things he is saying. The two find themselves gravitating to lunch.

When she asks him more about himself, she's astonished to learn of all that this young man has already achieved. And while it's hard for her to understand the technical jargon that he's suddenly spouting, a current of excitement jolts through her: she recognizes a skill that is needed for the planetary birth experience, which she has spoken of for so long.

She eagerly exchanges business cards with the young man and promises to send along some material she has written, specifically *The Evolutionary Synthesis*.

The name on his card: DARRELL LAHAM.

A Planetary Nervous System of the Soul?

As often happens, busy lives keep the two from connecting with each other again soon—not until, in fact, well over a year later at Hummingbird Ranch.

Barbara then learns more about Darrell Laham—that he is a cognitive scientist who has worked on a method of examining vast amounts of seemingly unrelated text to explore possible connections in meanings.

His work became "noticed," as they say, and was bought in 2005 for a substantial sum by Pearson Education, an international company that publishes textbooks, multimedia learning tools, and other educational material. That life event made Darrell financially secure . . . and in search of something to do with his brilliant mind.

Later still, while in Darrell's recording studio in Colorado, Barbara becomes clear that, applied to the thousand and one ideas placed on the Internet every day, software (such as the type that Darrell has created) could instantly find links between apparently disparate, but ultimately similar or harmonious, undertakings the world over. It could act as a planetary nervous system, keeping the Body Human abreast of what is going on where, and bringing it new vitality and unheard-of potential through the simple connecting of its parts.

In other words, it could do *exactly what Barbara Marx Hubbard has been dreaming of doing for 40 years.*

Had that first connection in East Lansing, Michigan, been just a "chance meeting"? Barbara can hardly think so.

And neither can Darrell, once he hears all that Barbara has up her sleeve.

≝ ≝ ≝

REFLECTIONS & EXPLORATIONS

The Intricate Design

As we reflect on the times just described, and look more closely at Barbara's experience to see what we all might benefit from, we are reminded that . . .

. . . there is no such thing as coincidence.

You can label what you've just read about as "coincidence" if you like, but the odds of two people—one with a vision of creating a way in which all the best ideas and newest innovations for making life work could be listed, categorized, and interconnected; and the other with the brainchild of a technology to do exactly that—finding each other out of the *six billion humans* on Earth at the precise time when *a third person* finds a million dollars from *a fourth person* with which to do it . . . are one in a *ka-zillion*.

Unless, of course, you're dealing not with "coincidence" at all, but with The Intricate Design.

Part of that Design, we see once again, is the interplay between emergency, tragedy, and opportunity. In this case, the posing of a question from son to mother that—because of the unforgettable moment in which it is asked—sparks renewed creativity and life even in the throes of death.

Can a person help a loved one from beyond the veil? Barbara Marx Hubbard believes so emphatically.

"Wade comes to me like a spark of light whenever there is something I need to get done," she told me as I was writing this book. "This is clearly more important to him than what *he* had to get done. Or perhaps this *is* what he had to get done. Perhaps he came here, in part at least, to support me. He always was, it seemed, more interested in what I could do than what he could do.

"We all come here to help each other in some way, don't we?" she asked me rhetorically on that day at my house in 2010. "I mean, here you are, helping me complete my mission by writing this book. And I should imagine that I've helped you along the way."

"Oh, yes, Barbara, you have," I assured her. "Even as you've helped others believe in their own gifts; to search for them, find them, and share them with the world. Even as you'll help even more in seeing, recognizing, and appreciating the miracles and serendipities of their lives, by telling us of yours."

Further reflection on Barbara's intricately interwoven life causes us to be reminded that . . .

. . . sometimes ideas precede their highest application.

This is not a small realization. Please don't glide over it lightly.

I'm saying that Life does not always present itself in a logical sequence. So never, ever, dismiss an idea as having no practical application in your life simply because it appears to have no application *right now*. Every idea has *much* to offer, or it *wouldn't have come to you*.

You know, of course, where ideas come *from*, yes?

Of course. They come from The Source.

The Source of what?

The Source of all wisdom, of all clarity, of all creation, of all innovation. Indeed, The Source of All Life, of All That Is.

We honor that awareness when we pay attention to what Life is bringing us. Great ideas may, as I've just noted, not only occur to us days, weeks, months, or even years prior to their having any practical application, but also far in advance of when their highest application may even be *possible.*

Could this have been what happened to Darrell Laham? Could his ideas about what he called *deep semantic analysis* have "come to him" before he actually knew what their highest application was going to be?

Could this have been what happened to Barbara Marx Hubbard? Could her ideas about a Peace Room have "come to her" years—decades even—before she actually knew what their highest application was going to be?

I'm suggesting to you that the answer is *yes.* And I'm suggesting that in this particular case, the *relationship between these two ideas* was a *compelling force* that drew these two people together in the first place.

This is how and why people enter each other's lives.

They arrive with an apparently separate agenda, only to discover that the magnetic attractor that drew them together had to do with a conjoined agenda—unknown to them at the start, but made clear to them very soon, through the remarkable and synergistic process of Life itself.

I'm saying that this is happening in *your* life right now. The people and ideas that have come to you are all part of The Intricate Design. The Universe wastes nothing, least of all motion.

You will see this truth play itself out on the pages ahead, as we explore more and more of Barbara's story.

Enjoy.

✤ ✤ ✤

12.

EPISODE #17: DEATHLY DIAGNOSIS, OCTOBER 2005—
Nearly Two Years Before "a Chance Meeting?" . . .

Barbara is being driven by a dear friend, Carolyn Anderson, to Palm Springs, where she is to receive a Lifetime Achievement Award from the Association for Global New Thought and will deliver a major address in the form of her acceptance speech.

It's a beautiful day, and Barbara is enjoying the drive and good conversation with Carolyn. Their lively exchange is interrupted by Barbara's cell phone.

"Mom, it's Wade."

"Wade! How *are* you, darling? I'm just on my way to Palm Springs to—"

"I've received some interesting news, Mom."

The concern in her child's voice is evident. "About what, sweetheart?" There is the slightest pause. "About what?"

"I've just been diagnosed with a major tumor." Barbara catches her breath. "They say it's fatal, but I don't believe it."

"Oh, Wade . . . where *is* it?"

"It's a brain tumor, Mom." Now she turns white. "They call it *glioblastoma*."

Barbara doesn't know it in this moment, but in the medical profession, they describe this condition with three words: "Death on diagnosis."

Untreated, the average patient lives three months, and with treatment, one to two years. According to Wikipedia, "the single most prevalent symptom is a progressive memory, personality, or neurological deficit due to temporal and frontal lobe involvement."

Shortly, Wade will begin exhibiting all three. At this point, though, none of that is happening. Wade sounds perfectly fine on the other end of the phone—and very determined.

"I want that tumor out," he says.

Barbara tells him that of course she supports him in that, and will do everything in her power to see him victorious in the battle they both know lies ahead.

Wade hangs up, and Barbara tells her friend at the wheel what she has just heard. Silence descends. Carolyn reaches out and holds Barbara's hand as Barbara weeps softly, fear and sorrow creeping into her consciousness like a disease of her own.

Within hours, she is to speak on the future potential of humanity, and now she will have to do it knowing that her own son's future potential is, perhaps, extremely limited.

He is in no immediate danger. If he were, she would cancel the appearance and race to his side. But this is not the case, and they both know it. So Barbara pushes onward and makes the presentation—although what was expected to be a lighthearted and thoroughly joyous occasion becomes an extraordinarily challenging one.

Embracing a Larger Truth

During her speech, Barbara doesn't elaborate about Wade's circumstance, but she does reframe her remarks in the context of tragedies that are occurring in the lives of so many people in so many ways at the same time that many new possibilities are being born.

"Concurrent realities, I call them. They create the terrible dichotomies within which so many people now live," she tells her audience. "The only way that anyone could hold a positive vision of the future would be to see our present-day circumstances in spiritual terms."

She pauses for a moment, clearing emotion from her throat. "Many are dealing on this day with tragedy, pain, and suffering. And Life invites us to call up the deepest faith, an inner 'knowing,' that crisis precedes transformation, problems are evolutionary drivers, and nothing happens that does not also have a greater meaning."

Her audience is moved, but can never know the emotions that are competing inside of Barbara in that moment. Once home, she immediately calls Suzanne Mendelssohn.

"I'm afraid I've had some bad personal news, and I'm hoping you can help me." She explains about Wade.

She would never have had a reason to call Suzanne about Wade if she had not once called Suzanne about *herself* three years earlier. And why would she have called Suzanne at all? Well, she never *would* have, had she not met Edgar Mitchell many years before *that*—all of which set the stage for Edgar to lead her to Suzanne, and for Suzanne to lead her to the man on the phone in the hospital . . . who himself first touched Barbara's life 30 years before!

So why would Edgar Mitchell lead Barbara Marx Hubbard to Suzanne Mendelssohn two and a half years before Barbara found out about her son's illness? Ah, yes, the tapestry again . . .

EPISODE #16: AN ILLNESS BECOMES A HEALING, JANUARY 2003—More Than Two and a Half Years Before the Deathly Diagnosis . . .

This part of the story begins with a visit by Barbara to her sister, Pat Ellsberg, who lives a short drive from Santa Barbara. During this time, Barbara experiences severe internal pain. It subsides for a bit, but not altogether.

Concerned, and back at home, the discomfort has gotten worse, and Barbara calls on her doctor.

"You know, from the symptoms and my examination, I'm suspecting there's something serious going on."

"How serious?"

"Serious enough to put you in the hospital right now."

The doctor tells her nurse to call Cottage Hospital and arrange for an admission at once. Barbara's eyes widen. "What's happening? What's wrong with me?"

"I think you have a ruptured appendix."

"What?!"

"I'm thinking you need immediate surgery. Not in a couple of days or a few hours. *Immediate.*"

And that's exactly how it goes.

The surgery is successful—but another problem is uncovered.

"Now what?" Barbara asks her doctor, just a little exasperated.

"Your white blood cell count is abnormally high. We need to run some tests."

When the results come back, the doctor looks even more solemn than when Barbara first came into her office with the ruptured appendix.

"Barbara, I'm going to give it to you straight and fast. You have chronic lymphocytic leukemia."

"Is that . . . is that a form of cancer?"

"Yes. It's not immediately life threatening, but it's not good."

The Road to Self-Healing

Barbara is taken aback: *This is not my disease! Why would I have this? What is going on here?* She gives herself time to fully recover from the appendix surgery and then heads off to Hawaii. She has heard of a woman there—someone who might help sort things out and maybe even turn things around.

Shivani Goodman had spent six years with the great Indian master Babaji and has held off the effects of breast cancer for years following her diagnosis. Barbara has heard her explanation of how she has done it: "Through the deep inner work of reviving the loving and dynamic nature of the Self and its ability to impress upon the subconscious images of health and wellness."

(Shivani ultimately died from the disease, but in victory *over* it, having lived healthily and vigorously far longer than most people might ever dream of, given standard medicine's prognosis.)

Meeting for the first time, the two feel immediately comfortable with each other. It's as if they've met before. Shivani encourages Barbara to "work on the 'codes,' or toxic attitudes, that you might still be carrying with you, which could be triggering this illness."

Barbara knows exactly what this is about. Thoughts such as *I'm a failure* visit her regularly, as do the words she'd heard from her father: "You're a crazy fool. This will never work."

She tells Shivani that she also felt that she was "never finishing my assignment."

"Let's go underneath and find the beliefs that are causing these toxic thoughts," the healer offers. "Then we can begin—thought by thought—to 'recode' your subconscious with chosen thoughts, ones that evolve you."

Ultimately, new thoughts are selected, such as: *I'm fully grateful for the way the process is unfolding* and *There is nothing more that I have to do.* With each new code, Barbara feels herself lightening up. "Those other thoughts feel like invisible strings, binding me to the heaviness of my past," she shares.

"That's exactly what they are. That's a very good description," Shivani remarks.

Barbara has a sensation of rebuilding her body cell by cell, thought by thought. She is fascinated by the experience and wonders: *Does conscious self-evolution mean that we actually do self-evolve through conscious intentional thoughts?*

Characteristically, her mind now begins to race.

Do we create ourselves by our word? If we are members of a self-creating universe, does there come a time in our evolution when we become self-creative of ourselves? Are we shifting from the animal-human life cycle to a universal life cycle, just at the time of the planetary birth? Am I really one of the many "mutants" of the new species of humanity? Or is this simply the natural growing up of a very young human species? Or could it be both?

"What's going on over there?" Shivani asks. "What are you feeling?"

"Well," Barbara responds, "I feel like an imaginal cell that has been in the body of the caterpillar and is now actually living in the body of the butterfly."

"Wonderful! That's perfect."

A few days later, Shivani takes Barbara through a past-life regression. Presently, Barbara, eyes closed and completely relaxed, seems very far away.

"Where are you?" Shivani asks quietly. "What are you seeing? What's happening?"

"I'm in the Elysian fields of Greek mythology. I'm the same Universal Being—a human light body—that appeared to me in Montecito as my higher self, my future self. But now she is . . . I am . . . in the past. This means that we are *eternal.*"

Barbara says nothing more for a moment, but Shivani can see her eyes moving behind closed lids. It's like the REM (rapid eye movement) of very deep sleep.

Now she speaks again, slowly, almost in a whisper.

"I'm at the outskirts of the field. This is where the ancient masters dwell. I can see vague outlines. There are women in flowing robes and men with long beards . . . they look like Plato and Socrates. I'm part of a group—part of this group. Wait, something is happening. . . .

"Oh, my goodness . . . we are all volunteering to come to Earth together to facilitate the birth of a universal humanity. Our task—okay, wait . . . yes, we agree, we understand that our first job will be to find each other."

"How?" Shivani softly inquires. "How will you do that?"

"Through attraction and resonance. Each of us holds a part of the Plan. None of us can fulfill his or her part without finding enough of the others."

Barbara breathes peacefully and deeply, her face becoming as smooth as a baby's. Nothing more is said. Shivani leaves her in that quiet, peaceful place for a while and then gently brings her out of the regression.

That night, Barbara writes this in her journal:

"It is my assignment now to notice whom I'm deeply attracted to, and who is attracted to me. I'm to be with these people in depth, with no agenda except to ask them these questions: *Do you remember having volunteered for this task? What do you know about the Plan? What is your part in it? What do you need to accomplish it?*"

In the years that follow, Barbara would ask these questions of many people—particularly those she often found herself collaborating with. It was a rapid and efficient method by which she could identify who her co-creators would be at this stage of her life.

Now you might say: *This is interesting, but what does it have to do with Edgar Mitchell leading Barbara Marx Hubbard to a woman named Suzanne Mendelssohn? And why would she be thinking of calling this Mendelssohn woman now?*

Wait for it. The mystery is unraveling.

🌾 🌾 🌾

13.

Returning from Hawaii, Barbara tells a friend about her time with Shivani Goodman. "I felt so light. She put me through an exercise of going backward through every year of my life, forgiving every wound I'd received or given to anyone, and detoxifying every negative thought that I could remember, right back to my birth and even *before* my birth. That's when I found myself in the Elysian fields. . . ."

Barbara recounts that experience, then adds: "The great thing about the work I did is realizing that all of us can detoxify the negative thoughts we're holding and substitute positive ones into the thought field of our being. This is a *rebuilding of the Self* from the level of our thoughts up. It leaves one in a place of real peace, of genuine bliss."

After that experience, Barbara asked the Universe a question: "'How can I describe this feeling and healing to others?' I was looking for a way to put what was going on with me into words."

"And . . . ?" Her friend inquires.

"I came up with a word. I was given one word that has made things very clear to me. It carries a lot of meaning for every woman on this planet, and I don't think I could pack it into any other single word."

"What is the word?" Her friend is eager to know.

Barbara smiles. *"Regenopause!"*

"Regen . . . I'm sorry—what?"

Barbara repeats: "Regenopause."

"That's a word?"

"It is now." Barbara's eyes twinkle.

"But you said it carries a lot of meaning. What does it mean?"

"After *menopause,* we have no more eggs. We *are* the egg! We are giving birth to our own feminine self. If we uncover and say *yes* to our spiritually motivated vocation, there is a pause in the aging process when we literally begin to *regenerate.* We don't age as before, and we're flooded with new energy and vitality."

Her friend's face reflects an I've-got-it "Aha!" and Barbara continues.

"I've never felt better in my life. If I had any doubt about living to 80 and beyond, *whatever* my so-called medical condition, those doubts have all been erased. In fact, the years ahead may be my most productive."

Barbara explains that a woman in *regenopause* is an element of the emergence of the new female of the species. And there is a corresponding element for males, she notes. It is *midlife croesus,* not *midlife crisis.*

"Men can go through their own kind of 'menopause,' you know," Barbara asserts. "Yet a man, too, can regenerate himself when he realizes that during the second half of his life, he need not be a male in crisis, his most powerful days behind him, but a wealthy man in the highest sense of the word: rich with achievements yet to come, mountains yet to climb, dragons yet to slay, and a planet yet to save. All he has to do is tap into the wealth of his own essential self, his own gathered wisdom, and his own ability to renew himself and his world."

Raising Eyebrows

Barbara says that she is "actually grateful for my ruptured appendix, my leukemia diagnosis, and all the illnesses that signaled me to go into regenopause."

"Wait a minute," her friend stops her. "You *go into* this regeno-pause? It's an act of will?"

Barbara nods. "This happens during the third Genesis, or third chapter in Humanity's Mystery Story; that is, when humans realize that we are co-participants in the process of creation, and that we are actually becoming capable of response—that we have 'response *ability*'—within the process of creation.

"When I'm silent and still, I can feel something unfolding, unscrolling in my solar plexus, all on its own, as if it were coded in. In the silence, I hear the message: *As an early mutant of the new species, I create a space for all of those who feel they are mutating from within to be together, resonant together with me and others.*"

Barbara watches as her words become eyebrow raisers. She has seen this occur before, and has learned to rapidly explain herself.

"What do I mean by *mutating?*" she asks rhetorically. "I mean *shifting in consciousness* from the illusion of separation to the experience of connectedness with each other, with Nature, and with Spirit. I mean being motivated from within by a new impulse to express unique creativity for self and world.

"All of my life I yearned for such a space in consciousness in which to feel normal. The world as it is didn't, and does not now, feel normal. It does not feel natural for us to be killing each other and destroying the environment. Now other beloveds and I have co-created such a space, a pool of self and social evolution. It is a Gateway through which you may come to make your transition in this lifetime—from your local, self-centered, self-conscious phase to your essential-self-centered, universal phase.

"It is a Gateway to become a member and builder of the new world. It is the space *of* the new world. This mutation has been occurring for hundreds of years in small groups—usually in mystery schools, monasteries, and ashrams—under the guidance of a spiritual teacher. Certain individuals, who are greatly advanced beings, have done it all on their own.

"Now this effect has finally reached critical mass. It is happening to countless members of our species from all faiths and disciplines, appearing not as a new religion, but as a new person, a new consciousness, a new yearning for the next phase of life."

"So the Gateway," Barbara's friend recaps, "is essentially a change in perspective, from separation to oneness."

"True, but more than that. Remember that I said it includes a spiritually motivated vocation and a new impulse to express unique creativity for self and world."

"You're saying we've got to find something to do in the second half of our life."

"Yes, but not just anything. Not stamp collecting or antiquing. There's nothing wrong with those things, but that's not what I'm talking about. I'm describing something bigger: becoming a member and builder of the new world.

"I see caterpillar imaginal cells becoming members of the societal butterfly. Now we need containers in which we come together and, through our interaction, trigger the new coding in each other. That is the work I'm talking about. I'm talking about all of us helping to *create the container.*"

"What does that mean?" her friend asks. "I don't understand."

"It means that we each create the space in our own lives for our richest, fullest development; and we each *use* our own lives to help create such a space for others. We listen to our own inner voice—we attune to our inner passion to create, to our callings or life purpose. We say *yes* to that within us. This Yes triggers regenopause. We make it possible and comfortable for others around us to realize their own fullest potential physically, mentally, and spiritually. We provide the space for that to happen, individually and collectively.

"The Gateway to Conscious Evolution is such a container."

The Path Less Taken

Whereas some might have found a late-life diagnosis of chronic lymphocytic leukemia to be depressing, Barbara actually finds it reinvigorating. She has returned from Hawaii not only deeply healed but also deeply motivated. She is determined to empower and enhance her "regenopause" experience. She wants to remain healed, stay healthy, fulfill her life purpose, and *regenerate herself* for the years ahead. She has no intention of slowing down, much less calling it quits, at 73.

She phones a longtime acquaintance—Edgar Mitchell. She met the former astronaut in the 1970s when she was interacting with America's space program. Later, he attended several conferences and programs that she'd created. While they never qualified as close friends, the two clearly hit it off and enjoyed each other's minds.

She remembers now that Edgar had been diagnosed several years earlier with all the signs of liver cancer and had found energy healers to whom he went for consultation. Edgar had told many that the work of those healers, across long distances over a period of months, actually altered his prognosis, eliminating any signs of cancer in his body.

"Hello, Ed, it's Barbara Marx Hubbard."

"Why, hello, Barbara. It's been awhile. How are you?"

"I'm well—in fact, I've never felt better. And that's why I'm calling you. . . ."

She tells Edgar about her recent medical situation—about her wonderful experience in Hawaii and her sudden awareness of regenopause. Then . . .

"I've heard about your own experience with long-distance healing, and I was wondering if you knew anyone you might recommend to me so that I may continue my healing. I don't feel in the least that my condition is life threatening; rather, I feel as if I really am now *in* regenopause. But I want to make sure that I hold the focus and keep the process going. If you know of anyone I might work with . . ."

"I do know someone," the former astronaut replies. "She's always very busy, and I frankly don't know if she has the time to begin working with someone new, but I can certainly find out and get back to you."

"That would be wonderful, Ed, and I would be grateful. What is her name?"

"Suzanne Mendelssohn."

⁂ ⁂ ⁂

14.

And so The Intricate Design is at work once again. As a result of Barbara's chance acquaintance with a former astronaut, another connection is made; another player is brought onto the stage.

Barbara learns that Suzanne Mendelssohn is not only a healer but also a science intuitive, seeking to demonstrate the existence of God at the level of quantum physics. Another of her interests is to bring humanity into positive shared contact with extraterrestrials.

Although Barbara has had no personal contact with extraterrestrials, it had always seemed to her that there must be intelligent life elsewhere in the Universe, and she felt that the planetary birth experience would reveal whatever is actually true in any event. We will have to "grow up to find out," she always said. She finds herself impressed and fascinated by Suzanne, who has told Edgar Mitchell that she would be happy to work with Barbara.

Through this process, Barbara and Suzanne strike up a telephone friendship that continues through the years, even though, as noted before, the two have never met in person.

Thus it was that in April 2009, Suzanne reached Barbara in Boulder in a call from her Shelter Island home in New York, asking that million-dollar question.

Thus it was that, less than 24 hours later, Barbara—in the Boulder home of Darrell Laham to lay down the voice track of *The Cosmic Family Reunion*—would casually mention Suzanne's call.

And thus it is that, seeing it all in hindsight now, the "players" on this "stage" realize that this improbable sequence of events was clearly all "meant to be"—because if anyone had the *technical knowledge* to build the Peace Room and the ability to do it, it was Darrell Laham. All he would need would be, say, er . . . a million dollars.

Yet none of these possibilities or interconnections revealed themselves in the "here-and-now reality" of any of their lives prior to Barbara's "chance" exchanges with both Suzanne and Darrell— to say nothing of the man who was to call Barbara while she was spending hours in that hospital bed in Los Angeles wondering what she was doing there.

Obviously, we see now, she was there (she had found a way to stop the virtually ceaseless motion and activity of her life) to think, think, *think*. To ponder. To assess. To determine where she *did* fit into the overall scheme of things, to clarify in her own mind her role as the Teller of the Story in what she was certain would be the coming birthing of humanity. And to ready herself philosophically, psychologically, and metaphysically for a call from a man who had crossed her path 30 years previously, and who was now going to make available $1 million so that the role she saw herself playing could, in fact, *be played*.

And that's how a "mystery story" works. The pieces are falling together right in front of our eyes, but no one *knows* they are falling together until they all *come* together.

Putting the Pieces Together

So now let's go "back to the future" for just a bit, returning to that day in November 2009—just two months before the writing of this biography began—when Barbara was in the hospital in Los Angeles.

REVISITING EPISODE #23: THE CALL THAT IGNITES DAY ONE, NOVEMBER 16, 2009— A 30-Year Circle Closes . . .

The man on the telephone is Michael Tanner, and he was connecting with Barbara at just the right time—a time when she could deeply feel exactly what was happening and why; a time when she would be receptive to Michael's own early ideas and concepts for what he was calling "Day One"; and a time when she would be ready at last to step into the climactic scene of a lifelong dramatic script that would see her sharing with the whole world what she had foreseen a half century earlier.

Michael Tanner had only a brief conversation with Barbara on that day. He knew when he telephoned that she was in the hospital, so he just checked in to offer his wishes for her speedy recovery, then quickly suggested that he call her back after she'd been home a few days.

Still, he was on the phone long enough for Barbara to realize that this was "real." This crazy, against-all-odds confluence of events was actually happening. For it was during that hospital-room telephone exchange that Barbara was reminded that this man with access to the million dollars *had crossed her path before.* Improbably, she had met him *30 years earlier,* when he was a volunteer producer for the World Symposium on Humanity in 1979—an event at which she was the primary speaker.

What kind of coincidence, what kind of "closing of the circle," is *that?*

Of course, we know that there is no such thing as "coincidence," and life shows us time and again that every circle—*every* one—is ultimately closed.

(Indeed, it turns out that Michael Tanner *and I have crossed paths before,* years ahead of the writing of this book, at an event I was speaking at in Phoenix, Arizona!)

So Who Is This Man?

Michael Tanner is a technology developer and marketer whose experience spans more than 40 years, ranging from innovative media technology start-ups in consumer and professional audio to video dispensing systems, video on demand, home-theater sound, and digital-image processing.

He is also the founder and CEO of a technology incubation and licensing firm focusing on the work of outstanding partner-inventors of advanced technologies in energy, communications, and materials. Projects fall under the "Advanced Science Made Practical" banner and include on-demand hydrogen systems, landfill gasification systems, and "morphing" or shape-shifting technologies; as well as innovative imaging systems for cancer and other medical diagnostics.

In addition, he has played a key role in pioneering efforts to advance pollution-free energy systems, including "zero point" and "direct conversion" devices and scalable nuclear fusion technologies.

And now he has called Barbara Marx Hubbard—and it was not simply to renew old acquaintances.

But again . . . let's not get too caught up in trying to track the names and events here. Remember what I've been saying: it's not about that. I've already told you, anyway, how this story ends; how Barbara and Michael collaborated with many, including Darrell Laham and others, to create the global Day One event on December 22, 2012, launching the Synergy Engine.

Now it's time to tell you, in the words of iconic newscaster Paul Harvey, *the rest of the story. . . .*

REFLECTIONS & EXPLORATIONS

Are Lives Predestined?

As we reflect on the times just described, and look more closely at Barbara's experience to see what we all might benefit from, we are reminded that . . .

. . . there is an Intricate Design in your life, too.

Could it be true? Is there such a thing as "magnetic attractors"? *Are* the people and ideas that have come to us all part of an Intricate Design? At least some of them?

I believe the answer is *yes.*

Does that mean our lives are predestined?

No. I'm clear that we have Free Choice. We can make any decision along the way that we wish. Yet the Intricate Pattern is so complex and sophisticated that it can accommodate any decision we make.

For instance, each of us has met thousands of people in our lifetime and crossed paths with millions. We've had a billion times a trillion individual ideas as well. Life, it seems, is "setting us up" to produce any one of a countless number of outcomes based on our moment-to-moment choices. The fact that it is doing so is usually hidden . . .

But not always.

Alex and Donna Voutsinas, a Florida couple, met at work, fell in love, got married, and have had three little boys between their nuptials in 2002 and the writing of this book in 2010. The two tell the story of how they were sitting down together a few days before their wedding eight years ago to look over some family photos. They wanted to create a slide show for their reception.

At one point, Donna pulled out an old Polaroid of herself with her family at Walt Disney World in 1980. She was five years old.

Something caught Alex's eye. Looking at the picture more closely, his eyes widened. There, in the background of the snap-shot of his fiancée when she was five, was his own *father.*

Wait. It gets better.

His father is pushing a stroller, in which is seated—you guessed it—*Alex.*

The groom-to-be couldn't believe his eyes, so the couple rushed off to his mother's house, where they asked her to get out her own collection of old photos. Searching through the pile, they came across some snapshots taken at Disney World 22 years earlier. Sure enough, Alex and his father are shown in those pictures wearing the same clothes as the man and child in the background of the photo of Donna and her family.

Husband and wife had been in the same place at the same time, *within feet of each other,* and caught in the same photograph more than 20 years earlier, when they were toddlers.

It gets even more remarkable. At the time the picture was snapped, Alex and Donna lived in different countries—Alex in Canada and Donna in the United States.

They've shared the anecdote for years with relatives and friends, who never failed to marvel at the incredible story. Then one friend suggested they post the original photo on Facebook just for the fun of it. Soon other friends shared it with more friends—and before they knew it, three million people had clicked on the posting, and the couple had become world famous.

Now there are some skeptics who say that maybe Alex and Donna made the whole story up. You know, to get publicity and maybe a free trip to Disney World. I don't think so (it would be hard to doctor an original Polaroid photo). But do you know what? It doesn't matter to me. Because what I do know is that there are thousands upon thousands of stories just like that of the Voutsinases' that have been verified; and those serendipities, those miracles, those unexplained and inexplicable occurrences— such as Barbara's postdeath visit from Wade—remind me of one more of my favorite quotations from Shakespeare:

> There are more things in heaven and earth, Horatio,
> Than are dreamt of in your philosophy.

We will explore this truth deeply on the pages ahead, through the telling of more and more of Barbara's story.

Enjoy.

🌿 🌿 🌿

15.

What kind of "celestial magic" or Intricate Design brings a person to the hospital for one major medical condition (a bursting appendix is no laughing matter) and sends her home with another (chronic lymphocytic leukemia)? A condition that is serious enough to cause that person to call an old acquaintance, who leads her to a long-distance healer who, years later, opens the door to a man with access to a million dollars (a man who the hospital patient herself encountered three decades prior) and who reconnects with her while she is once again in a hospital?

For that matter, what prepares a person for the kinds of events and occurrences that place one in a position to co-create something like the Day One event of December 2012?

Where does one find the template for ideas such as the Welcoming Committee, the Peace Room, or the planetary birthing of humanity into the community of enlightened beings?

How does one generate the daring constructions and assertions in *The Cosmic Family Reunion*?

From what place comes the awareness—the consciousness—of such a Larger Plan?

Barbara Marx Hubbard has always been an amazingly vital, dynamic, expansive, imaginative, creative, and insightful thinker

—someone who is constantly coming from *outside the box*. Her gift for situational analysis is especially acute. Yet even this cannot fully account for the scope and sweep and magnificence of her vision. Something else must be at play here. Something else must be feeding her. And something else is . . .

The Morning of the Third Spiritual Encounter

Chapters 2 and 3 of this book contain the opening words of a dialogue that Barbara engaged in on August 23, 2002, with an inner source of wisdom and clarity that she ultimately identified as her own Higher Future Self—or, if you will, the part of Divinity that resides in her (and in every one of us).

I promised to get back to that dialogue (which has continued now for eight years) from time to time throughout this book. I would like to do so now, here in this chapter, because I think there's an important point to be made about Wisdom and Clarity itself, and about what kind of "celestial magic" is indeed at play here in Barbara's life—and in the life of all of us.

I think it's crucial to understand that one does not have to have an actual back-and-forth "dialogue" with an Inner Voice or Source in order to be guided, informed, inspired, and assisted by Life itself. In fact, I believe that Life is providing us with guidance, information, inspiration, and assistance all the time.

To me, Barbara's life demonstrates this vividly—and I believe that anybody's life would, if carefully examined. That's the point I've been seeking to make here. That's the Intricate Design I've been talking about: the design that produces what many of us call *synchronicity* or *coincidence*.

Further, I believe that all of us are capable of having the kind of actual dialogue that Barbara eventually had. And in her journal, Barbara writes about how we can do so—instructions from her own Higher Self. They were part of her first conscious communication with that Inner Voice, on the morning that changed her life.

REVISITING EPISODE #15: THE CONTACT, AUGUST 23, 2002—Returning to That Morning of Deep Connection, Five Months Before Barbara's Illness Becomes a Healing . . .

Barbara was in bliss. She had made contact. She had heard an inner voice before, but she had never experienced it like this, *as part of herself.* During what she called her Christ Experience, she felt she had heard the voice of the Divine Christed One. But that was tremendously different, radically different, from this. That felt like inspiration from another source; this felt like instruction from a source within and identical to, yet somehow greater than, her Self.

Of course, Barbara wanted to know how to make contact with this indwelling Self again. So she asked the question directly, and here is what the Inner Voice said:

> *Just focus on the joy you feel at the thought of a Universal Human partner on the Other Side of the Veil now offering a loving hand to bring you through. Feel in your solar plexus the joy and wonder that you already experience.*
>
> *You must stop and let us lift your vibrations. Refocus your integrated essence upward toward your full potential self on the other side of the transition. Ask for contact.*

Barbara replied:

> When I move into that state, I experience myself as a Universal Being, free of the field of Earth, ecstatic, a radiant flash of joy—like the sun breaking through the clouds. I'm omni-local. I have continuity of consciousness. I am both a unique self *and* a Universal Being. I am formlessness in form, not bound by my egoic self.

And her dialogue continued:

You will live out the myth in real time. You are to turn your attention upward in the developmental path toward your own potential self—not the Higher Self, who has just now incarnated, but the Whole Self arisen.

Just as you experience the resurrected Christ as the future potential of humanity in general, now you are to experience the arising human that you are becoming—specifically yourself as a real, live Universal Being always already present.

The myth you are experiencing is the myth of the fully risen Universal Human Self speaking to its rising earthly self to lift that self upward for the next level of union of the human and the Divine.

So *this* is the invitation, Barbara thought. This is the opportunity. This is what the birthing of a new humanity is all about. It is about "the next level of union of the human and the Divine."

Barbara now was given to understand that this was a two-step process: *the first is the union of the local and essential selves; the second is the union of the integrated earthly whole self with the risen Universal Self, an embodiment of its self in the future.*

The union of the "local" and "essential" self had been going on with Barbara for many years. This is that *calling* she has felt since she was eight! This is the calling *we all feel.* This is what it is all about.

Speaking of the dialogue that she was having with her Inner Voice, Barbara told me later: "I'm now convinced that it is a normal and natural advance in the inner work. It prepares you to be a fully Universal Human during the time of the birth of universal humanity. It opens you to the higher interdimensional (celestial) reality variously described throughout history as higher beings, angels, guides, entities, or UFOs.

"Now the thought here is that we are to incarnate those frequencies—embody them and evolve ourselves—in order to attract encounters with others who have already been born from their planetary wombs. Not aliens, but cosmic family."

Barbara's Higher Self felt at first like another being altogether, she said, because "its frequency was higher than my vibration as an essential self. The personal higher voice had been incarnated and had begun educating the local self. This prepared the field within me for the encounter with the Universal Self, which I believe every one of us has."

Because of the third spiritual encounter of her life that began on that August morning in Montecito in 2002 (and which continues to this day), Barbara said she "began the work of attempting to focus on the Universal Self and render those frequencies stable. I polished a little booklet called *The 52 Codes** taken from my journals and edited it into a workbook for people who want to become a Universal Human by incarnating that higher frequency."

≀≀ ≀≀ ≀≀

---

*Information on the availability of this booklet may be found in the Afterword.

The Plan and the Purpose

As we reflect on the times just described, and look more close-ly at Barbara's experience to see what we all might benefit from, we are reminded that . . .

. . . all of us have access to Universal Wisdom, Understanding, Clarity, Insight, and Creative Power.

To use our God-given access, we must enter into the "union of the local and the essential self." We must answer the *calling*.

If you turn back to Chapter 4, you'll see that I wrote these words:

Something is calling to you, and you couldn't ignore it if you wanted to.

I have a notion that this is a feeling with which you, yourself, may be familiar. It is a calling to create some-thing, to experience something, to *be* something greater. It is the calling of evolution itself, the deep inner impulse, the Grand Invitation of Divinity to rejoin It, to know It, to become It.

That passage may have slipped past you when you first read it, but I'm hoping that now it may take on a little more meaning. I'm suggesting to you here that what had been going on in Barbara's life prior to her actual dialogue has also been going on in yours.

The first step in achieving the outlook and inner awareness that can lead to eventual union with the Divine can be a years-long process (in some cases, decades long) for most of us, unless we have what is called a "Lightning Bolt Experience."

(My friend Dannion Brinkley actually had one *literally*. Others, such as Eckhart Tolle and Byron Katie, simply experienced a massive all-at-once awakening one day in which they saw and knew and deeply understood and felt that *nothing matters* in the way we all think it does; and they were, from that moment on, living from the space of their Essential Self, and moving toward the experience of their Universal Self.)

Barbara likes to say that she took the "slow boat" route, and that's what I love about her story and why I'm so happy to tell it, because as I've said now twice before, she's no different from the rest of us . . . and that gives me great comfort and lots of encouragement. I see that we all can experience our Essential Self and then our Universal Self, and all we have to do is surrender to the *calling*.

Not everyone does. Some people feel forced to ignore that inner yearning in order to "get on with" and meet the demands of "real life." Some people don't even know that the process is going on, not having had the benefit of exposure to material such as this that helps us recognize the signposts. And some people know very well that the process is taking place, but they are uncertain about how to respond to its calling.

Barbara's whole life has been a response to that calling, and that is the chief reason I find it so instructive. I see that what distinguishes Barbara from so many of the rest of us is her unswerving commitment and unending willingness to *do what it takes*—indeed, to spend a *lifetime* of doing what it takes—to pursue a different agenda. First, she sought to recognize the aspects of Divinity and then to call forth these aspects, experiencing them in her day-to-day life. And finally, to transcend these aspects and *become* them.

In other words, to Consciously Evolve.

This is The Plan. This is the Purpose of All Life: to Consciously Evolve.

I've put those words in capital letters because they are Very Important to Our Understanding of Life.

For many, Life does not seem to make sense. People struggle to put the pieces together, work out the puzzle, and find some rhyme or reason to it all. Yet the experience we are all having is not some random process. We are not passengers rolling around inside a runaway stagecoach. We stand upright in the chariot of destiny, drawn by the horses of our own vision, and we hold the reins of our experience firmly in our hands.

We will explore this truth deeply on the pages ahead, through the telling of more and more of Barbara's story.

Enjoy.

🌿 🌿 🌿

PART II

THE
PREPARATION

"I come to your story with these questions for all of you: Do you remember having volunteered for this task? What do you know about the Plan? What is your part in it? What do you need to accomplish it?

"I want you to let me know if you know. Join the global community to facilitate our birth as a universal humanity. Help to create Day One."

— BARBARA MARX HUBBARD

16.

I think it is significant that for Barbara Marx Hubbard, 10 of the 25 Most Significant Episodes in her life occurred in the final decade before the culmination of her work in 2012 with the Day One event.

That's an average of one major episode per year between the age of 71 and 82. What this says about the most opportune, rich-with-potential, powerful time of anyone's life is—I think—strikingly revealing. It may be *just the opposite of what we've all been taught.*

We've been living in a society that tells us it is *youth* that is the Prime of Life; a society that demonstrates that it holds the so-called elderly as having about as much to offer today's world as an empty, throwaway milk carton. But Barbara has been putting the lie to that idea since her mid-60s.

EPISODE #14: MOVING TO SANTA BARBARA, MAY 1999—
Three Years Before the Contact . . .

It is Mother's Day, and the Mother of Invention is offering a weekend presentation in Santa Barbara, California. (Barbara, of course, doesn't call herself that; that is what *I* call her!) She is sharing everything she has come to understand about Conscious Evolution.

As the event organizers put it, it is "the first time you can ever tell it as a whole." Instead of being a speaker at a conference or workshop, instead of planning events and writings books, Barbara is delivering her worldview to a community of people who can stay together long enough to discover what conscious evolution really is.

Barbara finds that idea amusing when she thinks about it now, because one year earlier, she had wondered if perhaps her work was finished. It's true that in 1997, she had helped create the Association for Global New Thought as a co-founder; and in '98, she'd developed what she called the "Emergence Process: The Shift from Ego to Essence" (recorded well in her book *Emergence*). But during a discussion for *this* book, she told me: "I thought that was going to be the end of it, the culmination of my work.

"I was a visionary and had expressed my vision in as many ways as I could. I was 68 years old, but I felt unfulfilled. It seemed I had achieved nothing of the 'assignments' I'd been given. I had this awful, nagging feeling of failure, of feeling behind, no matter what I did. Yet there was also something growing in me, something unnamed and still unknown. But I didn't sense that it was 'one more project'! No, it wasn't something I had to 'do.' It was my Self, evolving."

So now here she is, still carrying out her work but in a new way. She is focusing on her evolution. Still—ever the spiritual activist—she can't help but try to find a way to assist others in doing the same work simultaneously. And that is why, on this weekend in May 1999, she is keeping a promise that she made the previous October during a talk for the Mind & Supermind series, to which many of Santa Barbara's culturally creative and intellectually curious subscribe. She had spoken in that talk about the birthing and potential of humanity.

"My intuition," Barbara said then, "is that humanity is not heading for self-development but for self-evolution. Something new is being born in us because we are born at the time of a *macroshift* in the planetary body itself. We are like cells in the body of a fetus born during the ninth month. We are experiencing ourselves evolving during a planetary birth. Our new functions and capacities are being turned on. They feel like the frustration and desire to do and be more. This is not only personal; it is also a planetary story, a global reality."

The audience was enthusiastic, and as her presentation was ending, in an unplanned, spontaneous moment, Barbara asked: "What would happen if this whole community were to experience its own potential for conscious evolution?" That very night, 185 people signed up to discover the answer.

Within days of those sign-ups, a seed group formed and Barbara, who was then living in Marin, agreed to return to Santa Barbara on Mother's Day to spend an entire weekend presenting the story of what she called Humanity Ascending. In the interim, she visited Santa Barbara frequently to work with the seed group.

"I felt a remarkable resonance," she told me. "Each person seemed to be emerging in his or her own way. I shared the ideas about the coming of the Universal Human. My own experience was echoing back throughout the experience of others. I fell in love with everyone."

From that group, a larger community emerged, and people began using what Barbara referred to as "the SYNCON Wheel" (later to become the core of the Synergy Engine) as a symbol. Folks created core groups, its members attracted by their own evolutionary impulse toward what they called the "Universal Human"—the co-creator of new worlds.

Barbara asked them if they would work together for a year or two to explore the new path of self and social evolution. The response was overwhelmingly positive, and the first conscious evolutionary community formed.

This was it, Barbara decided. It was her first real chance to place on the ground, in day-to-day environments and situations, elements of the message that had animated her life for decades.

A Major Life Shift

It's said that the most exciting lives are led by those who are ready to move with the energy of the moment—to "go with the flow"—and that has certainly been one of Barbara Marx Hubbard's greatest advantages. She has that ability and willingness. She has always been light on her feet, and here she was again, dancing to the tune of the Muse.

She was off to Santa Barbara, taking a nonprofit foundation she had created, her life's work, and her life companion with her . . . just like that.

"Evolution usually works in small incremental steps," she wrote in her journal at the time, "but occasionally, it takes quantum leaps into discontinuous, radical newness.

"In macrocosmic evolution, this is called 'punctuated equilibrium.' Sudden jumps also occur in our microcosmic lives, activated by years of subtle events, which cannot be understood until the jump occurs. Then it can be seen from the other side of the leap that everything that happened needed to happen."

And again, deeper into her notes, we find a testimony to moving with the impulse that enlivens. . . .

"I've learned that it is vital in the early days of our emergence to follow the 'compass of joy' through the darkness of our confusion. It will lead to fulfillment if we will only stay the course. . . . I've found that my heart's deepest desire for more life, higher consciousness, and greater freedom has never guided me falsely.

"I give thanks that I've followed the profound passion that led me from my agnostic background to my years of wife and mother, to my early years as a visionary futurist, to this threshold at the dawn of my seventh decade, at a new beginning. 'Follow your bliss,' as Joseph Campbell tells us. It is the light to guide us through the night into the brilliant Sunlit Garden of Co-Creation where the future begins."

While living in Marin, Barbara had established a daily practice, and she wanted to share it with her new community. She had created what she called her Inner Sanctuary, where no distracting thought was allowed. "It is a field of pure white light in which I'm safe from my own 'to-do list,'" she explained.

Every morning she rose early, lit a fire, turned on a CD of chants, burned some incense, and sat in silence. There was no particular agenda—no need for anything specific to occur. There was just the sitting, the simple being. She placed her focus on the *feeling* of receiving guidance from her own higher self. Not the guidance itself, but the feeling of warmth, wholeness, goodness, fulfillment, joy.

The core groups in Santa Barbara loved the idea and were thrilled to have Barbara right there with them. They had a teacher, mentor, and model; and as they met, they experienced an affirming of the Innate Essence of each other.

As Barbara would tell me later: "We felt we were 'mutating' by being together, our coding being activated by the interaction of the 'two or more gathered' energy. We were an informal evolutionary circle, acting out the assignment I had received during the 'Christ experience'—a mandate to form just such evolutionary groupings."

(This isn't the first time that Barbara had mentioned the "Christ experience"—the second of her life's three major spiritual encounters—and we'll look at that event, in Barbara's own words, in the pages to come.)

Setting the Intention

Now offering an inspirational sharing with members of the core groups in her new home community, Barbara declares: "Our intent is to bring forth 'the Christ of the 21st century,' not as a religion or a church but as a circle of souls activated to become the Universal Human themselves.

"I know that to some, this may sound like blasphemy, but it was Christ himself who urged us to follow in his footsteps. And when his disciples were astonished by how he was living and what he was doing, he said: 'Why are you so amazed? These things, and more, shall you do, also.'

"So don't be amazed today. Something new is happening here. The Path of the co-creator is inclusive of, but different from, the path of the mystic or the God-realizer. We are not heading vertically to God. We are seeking to *incarnate the Divine,* and then express that essential creativity *in action,* to heal and evolve the world and ourselves.

"We have not seen a full model of what we are becoming, because none of us has ever lived through a planetary birth wherein we've made it to that new level . . . ourselves evolved in a new society, a co-creative society, with all our new technologies operating harmoniously, in an earth/space environment, in which everyone is free to do and be their best. But that is our goal, that is our invitation, that is our possibility.

"I'm not saying this is going to be easy. We happen to have been born when our planetary body as a whole is struggling to coordinate itself and cooperate as a planetary culture. None of our institutions is prepared for it. The ones who will do this are ourselves! We can be the evolving spirit-motivated co-creators!"

The energy in the room is palpable.

"The key here," Barbara continues, "is how to incarnate the Divine *and* express ourselves in the phenomenal world at the same time as co-creative humans—without losing connection to that inner Divinity.

"Most of us don't live in ashrams or monasteries. We are in the world, of the world, co-creating the world. It can be exhausting and disappointing, unless we can secure that Inner Connection. So that's what this is all about. That's why we're here together."

Stopping Is Not an Option

Even as she was beginning her work with the community in Santa Barbara, she had been asked to write a curriculum for conscious evolution by the Emerson Theological Institute, the educational arm of the Affiliated New Thought Network.

In her apartment in Marin, Barbara had drawn a huge evolutionary spiral. Then she assembled every book that had ever inspired her and placed them in sequence, based on how they informed each turn of the spiral: cosmology, biology, history, current events—the evolution of every sector of society. She immersed herself in the memetic code of the conscious evolution of humanity.

Completing the curriculum in Santa Barbara, a personal project that Barbara called "The Gateway to Conscious Evolution" was born. The Gateway was a location on the Internet designed for everyone to participate with one another throughout the world in doing what the on-the-ground community of close-knit supporters in California was attempting to do: evolve the individual spirit and the collective energy, simultaneously.

The truth is that Barbara couldn't stop her work in the world if she wanted to. Her inner process has always been deeply connected to her outer world—and her outer experience has always been deeply connected with her inner world. Yet it is clear that in most recent years, from 1998 to 2010, Barbara's focus has been more sharply trained on pursuits of the Soul. She has shifted from the outer work of social evolution and the birth of universal humanity as a culture to the inner work of self-evolution as a Universal Human. Everything that came before was magnificent preparation, a kind of "in the field training"—as it is for all of us.

❧ ❧ ❧

EPISODE #13: A TIME OF PREPARATION, SUMMER 1995—
Four Years Before Moving to Santa Barbara . . .

Barbara is living in Marin County, California. She is 66 and restless. She doesn't know, in the moment, exactly what is gnawing at her, but she is aware that she hasn't accomplished all that she came here to do. As it happens, the culmination of her work will not occur for *17 more years* (with the Day One event of December 2012), but she doesn't know this now. She is preparing for this, but she is doing so without knowing it, without being aware of what lies ahead—or how long it will take to reach her goals.

(Few people imagine—past the midway point of their sixth decade—that their life's work will reach its zenith *15 years later.* So Barbara can be forgiven for being a little edgy.)

She has spent much of her life exploring the largest questions: *Who are we, really? Why are we here? What is the meaning of all the power we've been given, as sentient beings in a material world? What is our purpose and our future? Do we have a role in creating it, or are we simply members of an audience watching its own story unfold, without any ability to affect it?*

Remarkably, Barbara has come up with answers. Answers that make sense to her—and to a lot of people. Yet would the world at large be able to hear them—or even be interested?

Barbara explained her frustration two years earlier in a remarkable interview with Dr. Jeffrey Mishlove for his television series *Thinking Allowed:*

"I was like a tiny little person with a flag—'Hey! Look here!' I had so much good news that it was almost too much for people to take. I was a positive Cassandra. I wrote a letter to a thousand people; I started to network. But I didn't know the immensity of the task of changing consciousness."

Now, in 1995, she is even more familiar with the immensity of that task.

Not Much Time Left

She told Dr. Mishlove in her interview that "environmentalists tell us we that have 30 years at most to radically change our behavior or destroy our life-support system and go through a real devolutionary spiral. Now how would anything change so fast within 30 years? That's very difficult to imagine, knowing how slow we are.

"However, given the vast speedup of connections, our complex communication systems, and the fact that we're constantly impinged upon by awareness that we are connected, mainly in a painful way—through war, hunger, or environmental degradation—is it possible that the crisis is itself a 'trigger of consciousness'? And if enough of us choose to collectively shift that consciousness, even by *intention* (I think it's part of the human intentionality here), I believe that we could have an extraordinary effect on the collective consciousness of the earth."

That is what Barbara is attempting to create in the mid-'90s. She wants to *produce an effect*, to *have an impact*, on the "collective consciousness of the earth." And so in 1995, she sits down to write what she intends to be her most ambitious articulation to date: *Conscious Evolution: Awakening the Power of Our Social Potential.*

In it, she presents the new worldview of conscious evolution and the ways in which humanity might develop a spirit-based plan of action in order to transform the world through the cultivation of social synergy, thereby helping to repattern human lives.

In this same year, Barbara also writes *The Cosmic Family Reunion,* the allegory that would ultimately (although she couldn't possibly know it) act as a magnet that would draw Darrell Laham to her Peace Room project (to be renamed the Synergy Engine). It is this story that once again places the vision of humanity's next evolutionary step into the context of a "birthing"—the entry of our species into the community of Universal Beings who fully know who they are and who exercise completely their magnificent creative powers as manifestations of the Divine.

As she explains it, that birthing process is not predestined to produce a wonderful outcome—and that's what is so arresting about her oft-used analogy. Barbara Marx Hubbard is not one of those pie-in-the-sky, everything-is-going-to-be-all-right sandal wearers who sees nothing but sunshine in our tomorrows.

The "Birthing" Process

As she stated in her 1993 interview (and also shared with me in my kitchen in 2010): "Birth is dangerous, and nothing is guaranteed. You can have a very sick baby, a dead baby, a baby whose birth ends the life of the mother, or a healthy baby.

"Now, a planetary birth, in my understanding, is a time when the planet's technology links it up, when it realizes its limits to growth, when it can't go on growing in the womb, when it has to curtail its population growth, when it has to handle its own waste and stop using nonrenewable resources . . . all the stuff of the environment is natural, if you're being born.

"And if, let's say, a fascist idea takes hold, we could have a horrible birth and have Armageddon. On the other hand, if the people whose consciousness is shifting naturally to a whole-centered awareness, one that is more loving and ecologically sensitive . . .

if that were ever aligned on a planetary scale, in my vision, then there would be a planetary birth experience in which the collective mass of people would feel as one, freely and spontaneously."

Barbara made the same points in her book of the same year, *The Revelation: Our Crisis Is a Birth.*

Eavesdropping on more of that 1993 interview between Barbara and Dr. Mishlove, we find a connection, in Barbara's thinking, between humanity's birthing and the new child's "parent" . . . whom some of us call "God."

The Divine Connection

BARBARA: We have a 14-billion-year history, and I personally believe that as we head to the planetary birth, all people will see themselves as a unique aspect of the whole. Their cultural roots will be considered a gift to the future, but the real roots of all of us go back—not just to the big bang because that was the physical manifestation—in my understanding now, *to the Universal Intelligence.*

MISHLOVE: The Universal Intelligence—I think that's an important concept. If we are to look at solving the enormous problems we have—breaking free of well-entrenched deep patterns of oppression, of waste, of warfare, and of violence across the culture—it's going to require some kind of quantum transformation of consciousness; and it needs to happen in our lifetime.

BARBARA: That is the amazing thing. Here are my basic reasons for hope—and a lot of people don't see this, but I don't see how they can miss it, actually. If you look at the 14-billion-year history, it is a continuous rise of consciousness and freedom. . . . I mean from molecule to cell to animal to human to us. There is no earthly reason why it would stop here, with a group of furry bipeds.

We're only 50,000 years old as Homo sapiens. Do you realize whales are *millions* of years old? So we are very young as a species—and we look it and act it . . . we're a mess. We are actually just coming out of the mammalian stage. But if you add to our animal heritage, and even our spiritual heritage, our mind system, consciousness, and our technological social system, you actually begin to see the possibility of the birth of a universal humanity. That's my particular word for it.

MISHLOVE: You sometimes call it *Homo Universalis.*

BARBARA: Right. And I say that we come from Homo sapiens through a birth process where we are shifting from self-centered consciousness to whole-centeredness: cosmic-, Buddha-, Christ-, *God-centered consciousness.* . . .

Basically, each culture is patterned with an experience of a higher state of being, and everybody has heard it one way or the other. For example, take the pyramids in Egypt. They were really the beginning of the idea of the human becoming a regenerating god. In India, through the great yogis, they transcended self-consciousness through yoga, through union with the All. In Greece, we penetrated the visible world into the world of the invisible atom; in Israel, Abraham and God, the Covenant between humans and God for the transformation of the physical world—the New Jerusalem, the new Heaven, the new Earth. Could it be that all of those religions are ancient futurists?

MISHLOVE: Ancient futurists.

BARBARA: Yes. And then, when Buddha came in, there was a great individual that we actually have the story of, the history of, which represented human enlightenment. And then I believe when Jesus arrived, he represented a map of the total physical and psychological transformation of the human to a co-creator with God.

MISHLOVE: In other words, Jesus came not so much to be worshipped by us as something far above us and unobtainable, but as someone pointing the way and saying, "Come, be like me."

BARBARA: His basic reason for being is to demonstrate what we can do. And when he said, "You'll do the work that I do, and greater works than these will you do in the fullness of time," my experience is that this is true.

Even if we could look at our situation right now, we are doing the work that he did, and greater works, but often without the consciousness. Whether it be in our healing or our technologies, we can do Christ work, even now. But we're not yet in Christ consciousness as a collective.

And by Christ consciousness, I'm not talking about a religion. I'm talking about a consciousness that the source and the person are one: "The Father and I are one, and of myself I do nothing." *That* is what Jesus said.

When any one of us realizes that we are one with Source, with Spirit, with God—and That is flowing through us—then we, too, have those powers. This is what I believe.

(The previous text is excerpted from the "Planetary Birth" episode of the *Thinking Allowed* television series. See **www.thinking allowed.com/2bhubbard.html**.)

Laying the Groundwork

Looking back on it now, we can see that all of it—the whole Birthing Story, the entire idea behind the Synergy Engine, the complete vision of a new future for a new kind of human beginning to find and create itself following the 2012 Event, as well as our eternal connection with God—was coming together in Barbara's awareness. This knowledge was given articulation in her writings, talks, and in her on-the-ground projects during the period from 1989 to that morning when Barbara made "contact" in August 2002.

Not coincidentally, this period of renewed energy—following what Barbara called her "lost years" (1984 to 1989)—began with the entrance into her life of a most unusual man . . . an individual who would reenergize everything.

🌾 🌾 🌾

18.

EPISODE #12: LIFE MISSION REIGNITED, 1989—
Six Years Prior to a Time of Preparation . . .

Tall, handsome, slim, and elegant, with pure white hair, the face of a Roman emperor, and a cultivated voice brimming with "gnosis" from years of study and life experience, Sidney Lanier had been an Episcopal priest, had founded The American Place Theatre in New York as a church theater, and was now conducting the New American Place Salon in San Francisco with his wife, Jean Lanier. He was also working with Laurance Rockefeller's Fund for the Enhancement of the Human Spirit, giving away millions of dollars to transformational leaders.

At this moment in his 65th year, Sidney was on a plane to Jackson Hole, Wyoming, to meet a woman he'd heard of and with whom he'd become fascinated.

It was five years after Barbara Marx Hubbard's vice presidential campaign. Greystone, where she had lived in Washington, D.C., had been turned back over to her sister, who had lent it to her for 12 years to use as a base for a major project in social transformation.

Barbara's life companion, John Whiteside, with whom she lived at Greystone and founded The Committee for the Future in 1970, had died seven years earlier of cancer. Her children were all grown and away from home. She was on her own, and for the past five years, she floated from place to place, staying with friends who connected with her work on a very deep level and wanted to support her in its undertaking.

Barbara lived with her dear friend—global economist and author Hazel Henderson—in Gainesville, Florida, and then with other friends in Orange County and Northern California. Eventually she moved to Boulder, Colorado, where she occupied the downstairs apartment of a couple, Glenn and Marian Head, with whom she had co-founded a design center to develop ideas to produce social synergy, as well as market SYNCONS ("Synergistic Convergence"—meetings that featured the coming together of all vital elements of the social body to discover their functional relationships to each other and to the whole).

"It was a hard time for me," Barbara told me later, and that's why she called the period her "lost years." None if it, she said, "really felt right."

She described those moments more fully toward the end of her autobiographical book, *The Hunger of Eve*.

(*Author's Acknowledgment:* There are other descriptions of moments in her life that Barbara placed in this book. With her permission, I've occasionally quoted her in this portrait from that source.)

About those days following her vice presidential campaign, Barbara wrote: "I had no home base. . . . I could feel every element of self-importance dissolve. I kept ruminating over my past 'failed' opportunities to create an ongoing way to outreach into the world . . . none had manifested in enduring form. I felt deep pain. It seemed as if I had been on a mythical journey, with very large visions and goals. I felt like a complete failure."

Seeing Herself Through New Eyes

Things changed quickly in 1989.

It was then that Barbara was invited to a conference in Jackson Hole by the Together Foundation.

Sidney Lanier had read a book by Barbara titled *The Evolutionary Journey*, in which she described what she called the "Theater for the Future," and he was thrilled with it. It was a description of the whole story of creation, our crises as a birth, and insights into what it will be like "when everything we know we can do works!" as Barbara put it. It was what she called a "Preview of Coming Attractions."

Captivated, Sidney looked for everything he could get his hands on that came from Barbara. He pored over every sentence. Then he heard her voice on a cassette tape of some presentation or another, and that was it. He decided he had to find her somehow; he had to make a connection.

Sidney had been married to Jean Lanier for 30 years. He'd divorced his first wife, Nan; had left his role in the church; and begun a three-decade journey with Jean, who was a wealthy widow. Together they had created many exciting projects, including a personal-growth center in Spain and the New American Place Salon, a discussion forum that met regularly in their beautiful home at a marina in San Francisco. Now, Sidney and Jean were living together as brother and sister. She had another love in her life, and she and Sidney had come to an "arrangement."

Sidney knew that he was free. And now he wanted to find Barbara Marx Hubbard, this woman whose intellect, spiritual awareness, and sense of aliveness so intrigued him.

The Universe made it easy.

In yet another "noncoincidence" in Barbara's life, Sidney's employer, the aforementioned Laurance Rockefeller, "happened" to own the ranch at Jackson Hole where the conference Barbara was attending was being held. Sidney saw the flyer, learned that Barbara was among the invitees, and jumped on a plane immediately.

It didn't take him long to find her. She was in the grand lobby of the hotel where the conference was being held, wearing a bright red dress. Sidney went directly to her and introduced himself. "I've studied all of your work," he told her. "We must talk." He invited her to lunch, and she accepted. "The minute I saw him, I loved him," she confessed later.

During lunch, the conversation went deep very quickly. He repeated that he had immersed himself in her ideas, and then he said something quite unforgettable.

"I have a direct entry into your heart."

It was not a random comment. It was deliberate—and the purpose was to win her affection. He achieved his goal, charming Barbara completely. Sidney talked to her admiringly about her guiding thoughts: the unlikely combination of the "love of evolution; Jesus as our potential self; the coming role of the United States in the world as a place for the nurturing of the sovereign person, beyond all dogmas and separate ideologies; and the ultimate meaning of the space program," as she described them to me later.

Seeing herself through new eyes, another's eyes, Barbara was uplifted. She had been without a companion since John Whiteside's death, and she had, frankly, never expected to be with a man again. But then, there across the table, was Sidney . . . who, likewise, was smitten. He told her all about his open marriage, and that he and his spouse were no longer lovers; rather, they cohabitated only as best friends, remaining legally married as a convenience and out of long-standing camaraderie. This wasn't bad news for Barbara. It gave her a reason for going slow.

And so began an easy acquaintanceship—yet one ripe with possibility. Even at the very beginning, even at that first lunch, Barbara felt a reigniting of passion for her own work. And over the months that followed, Sidney's encouragement, his willing and ready ear, his excited and inspired reflections on her every thought, continued to raise her spirits after five years of doldrums.

‌ ‌‌ ‌*

19.

When the Wyoming conference concluded, Barbara returned to Boulder and took up her work with more energy than she'd felt in a very long time. She was traveling as a Soviet-American citizen diplomat and had recently returned from Soviet Georgia. She was also commuting back and forth to Northern California, collaborating with two former nuns, Jeanne McNamara and Linda Duffy, on editing and condensing an inspiration on evolution drawn from the New Testament that she had written nearly a decade earlier (titled *The Book of Co-Creation*). Jeanne had a home in Mendocino.

Barbara had long ago committed herself to a deep spiritual path. Having been dramatically impacted and inspired by what she has called a Christ Experience earlier in her life, she was guided to experience the Eucharist every day. The two former nuns joined Barbara in the ritual, feeling it as nurturing the work of helping form an ongoing Communion of Pioneering Souls of Earth through the actualization of the unique genius of innovative people with one another. In the Communion experience, she and her friends worked on overcoming the illusion of separation and feeling the "ecstasy of synergy or co-creation."

Simultaneous with the editing work in Mendocino, Barbara was creating a new book, articulating an evolutionary agenda that could lead to the transformation of the military/industrial/technological complex. In addition, she was flying to speaking engagements all over the country, telling the new story to all who would listen.

Unwittingly, Sidney had, with all of his encouragement, actually made it more difficult for himself if he wished (as he fervently did) to get close to the woman with whom he had fallen in love. She'd become a whirlwind, and it was difficult to stay personally close to Barbara. Sidney, however, had no intention of giving up.

He called her nonstop through the months, and she welcomed the intellectual and emotional support, sharing with him more of her ideas and even reading to him some of the newly edited parts of *The Book of Co-Creation*. He also visited her frequently when she was in Mendocino, joining Jeanne and Linda (who equally enjoyed his company) in exploring and testing every philosophical concept and intellectual construction Barbara had ever come up with. The exchanges were lively and stimulating—and time was flying, as it always does when people are in their element and celebrating their gifts.

The months turned into a year, and then two. The friendship between Sidney and Barbara became a solid and important part of both of their lives.

Changing the Stakes

On one of their mornings together in Mendocino, Sidney is speaking directly with Barbara, Jeanne, and Linda after the Eucharist ritual while all are still in an elevated state of being together, experiencing themselves as mystical members of the living body of Christ.

Partly as a result of these inspired exchanges and partly as a response to her own renewed passion and energy, Barbara decides to breathe new life into a nonprofit entity called the Cathedral of Action, which she had created eight years before (and which had gone dormant). She discusses this idea with the group and suggests changing the name to the Foundation for Co-Creation.

"Its first purpose will be to advance the publication of the newly edited *Book of Co-Creation*," she explains. "Then, it will see to its dissemination. Sidney, will you serve on a newly constituted board?"

It was unexpected, but Sidney responds without hesitation. "I will, if you believe it will be beneficial."

"I see you acting as a shepherd of the flock of pioneering souls," she says, and with a gentlemanly nod, he assents.

Barbara is feeling more and more that Sidney had been sent as a person who could truly help bring into being a new spiritual order on Earth: "a chalice for the spiritual joining of pioneering souls," as she writes in her journal. In another entry from that same period, she notes: "I spoke with Sidney Lanier last night. He really makes my heart joyful. He sees *The Book of Co-Creation* as providing an 'engine to give guidance to Western Civilization.'"

Barbara has been yearning for Sidney to join her in her mission; that he be not just an intellectual and emotional friend, but a partner in the work. Now he will be.

Later that year—over Easter weekend of '91—Barbara has returned to Mendocino to put the final touches on the long editing project and is sitting in Jeanne's little kitchen. It is cozy and warm. The house is near the ocean. Sidney is there, and she has already taken some long walks with him on the bluffs above the sea. She is falling more and more in love. . . .

The two have never come close to being sexual, but that is the least of what was on Barbara's mind. "I was feeling that I had found my spiritual soul mate," she told me. "It was in every sense a deep spiritual experience."

In the kitchen, Sidney is holding forth eloquently. When he was an Episcopal priest, he had been a brilliant man of the cloth in New York City. Involved in cultural as well as spiritual life, he formed The American Place Theatre to feature American playwrights. He was friends with his cousin Tennessee Williams. He was a frequent visitor to the famous Actors' Studio, and spent many evenings drinking with Richard Burton and other stars.

There was no denying that Sidney Lanier was an intriguing, intelligent, sophisticated, spiritually alive, and glamorous man.

And now, between sips of coffee, he is proclaiming loudly in the Mendocino kitchen that males should begin at once to support the emergence of the feminine. "Only the rise of true feminine power can save the world," he asserts, adding for emphasis: "This is vital."

Barbara has been listening intently. And to her inner surprise, she hears her own voice blurting something quite spontaneously and impishly: "Very good, Sidney! How about trying it out with me?"

For the first time in a long time—many years, actually—Sidney Lanier is without words. He is simply, plainly, and utterly startled. Then, recovering, he smiles.

"I will, my dear lady, take you up on that," he announces, almost as if he were a gentleman at court.

A breeze wafts through the kitchen from one window to another across the room, carrying the lightness of laughter from the quartet out to the ocean, and the moment passes. But not the thought . . . not from the mind of either of them.

Raising the Stakes Even Higher

Sidney returns to his home in San Francisco, while Barbara remains for a while in Mendocino. Was all this just her imagination? What would happen now? And, on a more practical plane, where should she live? She couldn't, after all, stay with her friends in Boulder forever.

There seems to be no center to her life. She is shuttling between Boulder, Mendocino, and her various speaking engagements throughout the country, while living out of a suitcase.

Sidney, meanwhile, wastes no time moving forward with his commitment—lightheartedly spoken or not. He decides to arrange a meeting with Laurance Rockefeller to request funds to spread Barbara's ideas of co-creation as a spiritual path.

Laurance was a traditional Christian, but has been inspired by the idea of the *élan vital* from the philosopher Henri Bergson; and now he is on the frontier of spiritual evolution, having already founded with Sidney and Jean the Fund for The Enhancement of the Human Spirit. Its purpose is to support spiritual and social pioneers, and Barbara's work would fit elegantly into that model.

Early in May, Sidney calls Barbara and tells her of his plans. "Will you go to New York with me and meet with Laurance?" he asks.

"Of course, if you think there's a chance he'll say yes."

"I think there's a very good chance," Sidney offers.

There is a slight pause.

"Well, then, we should go," Barbara fills in.

Another pause.

"Did you have a time in mind?" Barbara asks.

And yet, one more silent time lapse. Then, at last, something from Sidney.

"Barbara, I want to move in with you."

And now the tables are turned. It is Barbara who is without words. Sidney waits . . . but then he can wait no longer. He asks gently, "Did you hear me?"

"Yes, of course I heard you. But you're still with Jean. How could anything like this happen?"

"Jean and I can work that out. The only question is if you will do it. Would you be interested?"

Thus begins a conversation neither of them thought this call was going to be about. Still, it all seems quite natural. Barbara has already asked Sidney to serve on the board of the soon-to-be-reinvigorated Foundation for Co-Creation. Now they begin to conceive of a Center for Co-Creation, within which could exist a Temple of Co-Creation, a center of Cosmogenesis, a universe room, a template of templates, a cosmic chapel, and a Theater for the Future. Things are starting to sound exciting.

"We need to see Jean." Barbara breaks the flow. "We need to see her right away, and we need to see her together."

Sidney readily agrees.

The Meeting and the Offer

Sidney's legal wife has already told him that she encourages his relationship with Barbara. She wants him to be happy, she tells him. And so the visit between Barbara, Sidney, and Jean in San Francisco goes well—although nothing is said about the future. It seems indelicate for any of them to bring it up at this first meeting.

Not long after, Jean comes to see Barbara in Mendocino. They take a long walk together. Somewhere in the middle of it Jean says quietly, "Barbara, do you want to have a relationship with Sidney?"

The two stop and look at each other with the eyes of mature, later-in-life women who ask for and need neither explanation nor excuse for the discussion at hand.

"It's important that you know," Jean softly proceeds, "that if you do want such a relationship, you would be very good for Sidney. I want always to be his very best friend, but I need nothing more from him, and it would be wonderful to include you in that friendship. Would that feel good to you?"

Barbara's heart flies open. Jean Lanier is a brilliant woman, a theologian, poet, student of evolutionary spiritual pioneers, a benefactress, and a close friend of Laurance Rockefeller. In fact, it was through her friendship with Laurance that the Fund for The Enhancement of the Human Spiritual Helper had been established.

The two are motionless now, experiencing one of those you'll-probably-never-forget-this moments. Then Barbara simply nods, a tiny tear escaping. She is ready for a relationship now, and this remarkable woman, in her gracious generosity, is making it possible.

She writes in her journal on May 23, 1991:

> Amazing and wonderful things have happened. Sidney Lanier and I have become co-creative partners. We are here at the Sonoma Mission Spa having a divine time. His wife, Jean, has encouraged this relationship. (He is 67 and she is 71.) He is in love with me. Our relationship is still "supra-sexual" because of my hesitation, timidity, or lack of sexuality. I'm not sure which, but I'd live with him.

Turning the Page

And now Sidney and Barbara are in New York for the conversation with Laurance Rockefeller, which Sidney had arranged. Surprisingly, the part of Barbara's work that Laurance mentions funding is not the Theater for the Future, the Peace Room, or the SYNCONS, but publication of *The Book of Co-Creation*—the one thing she doesn't need help with. She has already attracted a publisher who was anxious to produce the work. But Laurance loves the material and sees it as catalytic in making the possibility of a Christ Experience real for all of humanity. Further, he sees Barbara as a powerful model, the template for a person who is committed to being spiritually self-actualized and self-realized.

Barbara and Sidney talk it over and come to the feeling that it might be better to accept the Rockefeller funding than go with a regular publisher, giving them more control over the project. They move forward enthusiastically now with the reinvigoration of the Foundation for Co-Creation, preparing it as a vehicle to receive the funds and get the book out.

They also begin to hatch more creative ideas. Sidney could call a "Planetary Pastors' Convening." It would demonstrate our potential to give our gifts to the cosmic child humanity. Barbara could speak as a planetary voice of the future, of the alternative to Armageddon being a planetary birth experience.

Their intense creativity is fusing.

"Let's go somewhere," Sidney suggests. "I want to be with you where we can really talk, just the two of us."

"Yes," Barbara agrees. "I think we need that kind of quiet space now."

They travel to Holderness, New Hampshire, where Sidney and Jean have a beautiful boathouse overlooking a shimmering lake.

The next chapter has begun. . . .

🌾 🌾 🌾

20.

May is coming to an end. The boathouse is a rustic, spacious place with wide windows and a long comfortable window seat spanning the length of those windows, looking out onto the lake.

Barbara is still doing a daily communion ritual. "Sidney was a little amused," Barbara confided to me when she related the story for this book, "but he went along with the ritual because of my insistence. I felt that we were really transubstantiating the wafer and wine. We were *incorporating* the living body of the Divine.

"After each daily ritual, when Sidney and I talked, I always wanted us to speak for at least a little while as we had before in the Mendocino house with my dear friends Linda and Jeanne, with the inner voice of inspired insights."

I tilted my head, indicating that I needed a little bit more on that.

"I never wanted the communion to end," she explained.

"But one day what was actually happening was that Sidney was thinking not of communion, but of . . . well, a different *kind* of 'communion.' As I innocently continued in my meditation afterward, Sidney actually left, undressed, and appeared to me naked!

"I was shocked. I hadn't seen a naked man since John had died seven years before. I was completely disconnected from anything sexual, but I didn't protest or draw away from him. He led me to the lovely window seat overlooking the lake, and we made love. It seemed, it *was*, very natural. You see, I was already in love.

"I had held a vision since my Birth Revelation in 1966 and re-created it onstage in The Theater for the Future in 1978. The Evolutionary Story in that program ended with an affirmation of the 'birth' of humanity. We are one, we are whole, we are good, we are higher life. Now, my vision expanded, and I felt that Sidney and I could become, symbolically, among the many humans who would represent the Second Couple at the Tree of Life. This is the tree of the power of the gods."

A Mystical Union

Once again, I didn't fully understand the reference, and I told Barbara so. I had heard the story of Adam and Eve, of course, but I couldn't pick up on "the second couple at the tree" analogy.

"Humanity was expelled from the Garden in the Genesis story," she said, "because 'they'—that is, the first humans—were heading for the Tree of Life. The Father God said that when 'they' reach this tree, they will be immortal. In other words, humans would be like the gods."

"And that is not what God wanted?" I asked.

"According to the story, no. God was, according to this mythology, a jealous God, and would have no others possessing such powers as His. And so, 'they' were expelled from the Garden and punished forever: the women to give birth in pain, the men to work by the sweat of their brow, and the snake to crawl on its belly.

"Now I had always realized that humanity *was*, in fact, gaining the power of gods, through science and technology. And because Sidney and I both had such a similar understanding of spiritual matters, because we both loved evolution and the whole idea of God, I fell in love with Sidney, not just the man (who was handsome, seductive, charming, and brilliant), but the archetype of the New Man.

"I saw us meeting at the Tree of Life, joining whole being with whole being, among the many co-founders of the new Family of

Humanity. There were other couples, too, who would have the wisdom to guide our new powers toward ever-evolving life rather than toward self-destruction.

"So I experienced that the joining with Sidney was in this archetypal realm. I began to see him not only as a man, but as a New Man; as Man Redeemed. He filled this role brilliantly with me in the archetypal realm.

"In the personal realm, we began to develop deep problems, but in the archetypal realm of this vision, he was my soul mate, and I dedicated my life to being a 'shared presence' at the Tree of Life."

"So you saw it as a mystical union, a spiritual union," I summarized.

Barbara smiled and nodded. "That's exactly how I experienced it. We set it as our goal to become co-equal co-creators, a second couple standing at the Second Tree, the Tree of Life, with others doing the same, anchoring the new way of being and the building of a new society equal to our spiritual, social, and scientific/technological capacities."

Rising at dawn the day after her first physical union with Sidney, Barbara writes in her journal: "Well, I've received a response to my prayer for a co-creative partner. It is Sidney Lanier. His life purpose and mine merge. We are exploring co-creative couplehood. I intuitively knew there must be such a model. Somehow Sidney brings me forward fully, and I, him. He says he loves my masculine 'logos,' and I love how he expresses his feminine side without losing his masculinity.

"We've broken the physical barrier. I've been celibate since John died in 1981. I've had literally no sexual desire. The whole thing seemed weird. During the first years with Sidney as a friend, I resisted any sexual contact, feeling almost afraid. But here at Holderness, it changed."

Still later she makes another entry in her journal about the new dimension in her relationship: "This has released my reserve. Over the past few weeks, I've been fully awakened sexually. I'm a sensual being. When we lie together in each other's arms, I feel a gentle and all-pervasive ecstasy. I sense my body becoming light. He stays with me all the time. I see that sexuality is not just a physical encounter; it is an ever-present reality when it's awakened.

"The whole universe is sexual, operating by attraction, every particle attracted to every other. Supra-sexuality, the joining of genius, does arouse physical sexuality, and lifts it into the light of full whole-bodied communion. I feel 'conscious joy.' The inner void is gone. The feeling of failure is gone.

"I feel as though I'm moving into the infinite. Sidney says, 'My purpose is Barbara.' He proclaims that he wants to provide a hearth for my flame, that he loves the logoic woman, and that the Divine masculine—the drive, the sense of purpose, the urgency of the mission—in *me* awakens the Divine feminine within *him*."

Not as Easy as It Sounded

Now the challenges begin. Barbara discovers that her complex relationship with Sidney may not go as smoothly as she might have hoped.

Jean Lanier has decided that she wants to form a "triad," and asks that Barbara move into their home (at least temporarily) in San Francisco in June. Not totally convinced that this is a good idea, but not wanting to give up on something lastingly meaningful with Sidney before it even has a chance to take hold, Barbara goes.

Immediately upon reuniting, the three are filled with creative ideas: to produce a Visionaries Video, to make a blueprint for evolution that could build new worlds . . . someone even suggested a Citizens' Summit on the beaches of Rio. It is a heady time. Yet the main questions for Barbara remain: *Where should I live permanently? How can I live in relationship with Sidney—if at all?*

Jean describes how happy she is when they were all together in the big house. "I feel lonely when Sidney and you are away," she says. She invites Barbara to live with the two of them always.

The three of them leave it there for a while. Barbara stays on at the house, but without making a commitment to a long-term arrangement.

By July, it becomes apparent to Barbara that Jean and Sidney need to clarify the state of their relationship. "If they are not husband and wife, what are they?" she writes in her journal. "They say they are brother and sister. I'm not Sidney's wife, either. I'm his twin flame, his cosmic complement. Our vow is to love and fulfill each other's purpose through the fusion of genius."

Jean doesn't want to divorce Sidney, and Barbara doesn't want to marry him in the old way, but . . .

"Both Jean and I feel very strange," Barbara's journal reveals. "The first night when I came to their home and slept with Sidney, he shuttled back and forth between both of us to be sure that Jean didn't feel displaced. Then the old mammalian programming kicked on momentarily between Jean and me—and both of us just wanted to leave."

By midsummer, Barbara concludes that the only thing that will work is divorce. Jean did not disagree. She offers Sidney and Barbara a place she has in Marin County, where they can set up housekeeping as a twosome.

And that's how Barbara Marx Hubbard and Sidney Lanier became an Official Couple. They never did become legally married, but they remained companions for 20 years, "eternally engaged," as they put it.

✍ ✍ ✍

REFLECTIONS & EXPLORATIONS

Everyone Brings a Gift

As we reflect on the times just described, and look more closely at Barbara's experience to see what we all might benefit from, we are reminded that . . .

. . . there is a direct connection between what is happening now and what is going to happen in the future.

When you see that connection—or at least when you know it's there—you look more deeply into each Now Moment, you value more fully each Present Person, and you embrace more completely Every Event of Today as the True Gift that each is.

Like Barbara's, your life is a Mystery Story, unraveling itself one clue at a time. Nothing that is happening Now could be happening were it not for what has happened Then. This is true of *every* Now and *every* Then. And so, we can say with accuracy: *Every now and then we see the truth.*

Were it not for Sidney Lanier's arrival in Barbara's life at a crucial point when, in her 60s, she was just about to drop her dreams, the eventual telling of the Story of Humanity's Birthing into the Community of Universal Humans may never have happened in any widespread sort of way. Barbara's lifework, her "assignment," if you will, would indeed have gone unfinished.

I said earlier in this book, in a previous Reflection, that for many, Life does not seem to make sense. People struggle to put the pieces together, to work out the puzzle, to find some rhyme or reason to it all. Yet the experience we are all having is not some random process.

I want to repeat that here: The experience we are all having is *not some random process.*

We are *not* passengers rolling around inside a runaway stagecoach. We stand upright in the chariot of destiny, drawn by the horses of our own vision, and we hold the reins of our experience firmly in our hands.

A man in San Francisco reads a book and hears the voice of a woman on tape—a total stranger—whose life he is destined to change. A woman with a vision of couples coming to a Second Tree of Life, modeling the archetype of the New Human, accepts an invitation from a gentleman at a conference to share lunch together . . . and embarks on a bold new embracing of a decades-old dream, leading to the culmination of her life's work more than 20 years later.

These unlikely events occur regularly in people's lives. The fascinating thing is that most of them don't know they are occurring. That is, they don't see them for what they are. We're looking at miracles every day, and we're *looking right through them.*

Sidney Lanier deeply impacted Barbara Marx Hubbard's life. He reignited in her the visions she had held for 30 years, but that had begun to fade into a Dream Not Realized.

Her mood was understandable following the experience of so many of her ventures, projects, and programs ending without reaching fruition, as well as the emotional and physical drain of her campaign for the vice presidency of the United States.

Particularly when that ended, Barbara felt finished, really and truly *through* with the way-out-there exploits, the uncommon strategies, and the far-reaching experiments that were all aimed at producing major social change in our time.

Sidney put her back in touch with the part of herself that *knew* she had come to this physical life for a reason, with a purpose, and on a mission that was bigger than just Get Through Life as Best You Can. He encouraged her to return to her magnificence and to accept for herself nothing less. Least of all would he let her set aside the possibilities for a better tomorrow that might emerge through her.

In short, he was a blessing to her, arriving at just the right time.

The miracles in our own life are those who support our own life's dream, appearing before us, waiting to be recognized. They are all around us. *They are all around us.* And the beauty is that in the recognizing of these miracles, we *actualize* them.

So look across the room right now at the people in your life. One or two of them, in particular, may be your "miracles." They could be a life partner, a co-worker, a boss, or a friend. Think of the individuals in your life right now, and ask yourself:

- *What is this person doing here?*
- *How did this person get into the room of my life, anyway?*
- *Was this all just happenstance?*
- *Am I seeing the gift, seeing the miracle?*
- *Am I <u>making it a miracle</u> by the seeing of it?*

The truth is that nothing and *no one* comes into your life without a gift for you.

We will explore this truth deeply on the pages ahead, through the telling of more and more of Barbara's story.

Enjoy.

🌿 🌿 🌿

21

EPISODE #11: THE VICE PRESIDENTIAL CAMPAIGN, 1983—
Six Years Before Life Mission Reignited . . .

It was crazy, of course.

Or *was* it?

Maybe it was a unique way to get some unique ideas across. Maybe it was a wonderful way to say some wonderful things and have them be heard at last. Maybe it was a powerful way to use the mechanisms of power to give power to some powerful new visions that could empower the world to create a *new* world where power was shared by all and *used* by all to light the sky of humanity's dream. . . .

Okay, Barbara thought. *I'll do it. I'll run for vice president.*

Not the First Time

Barbara had considered running for high elective office before. In fact, she'd twice thought about running for the *U.S. Presidency.*

Actually, the idea had been suggested to her several times through the years by Buckminster Fuller and other influential and well-placed friends, but she herself hadn't seriously considered it until 1976.

"I knew there was a potential within people that could be called forth to action to build a humane community," she explained later. "The act of running for President appeared in my mind as a sacred act. It had nothing to do with ordinary power, but everything to do with wanting to help trigger the action."

In the end, she wound up not getting into the race. Jimmy Carter was running, and she realized that she would be seen by the public as being somehow *against* him (and everyone else who would be seeking the Democratic Party's nomination), and the whole business of announcing oneself to be "better" than the others was anathema to her. She felt she was *different* but not *better*.

And so, in order to place herself within the realm of *ideas* rather than the realm of political *competition,* she decided to put together the elements of a platform that *anyone* could run on. She called it a Platform for the Future—and Jimmy Carter became President.

Four years later, Barbara contemplated making the run again, once more encouraged by others—including American political journalist, author, professor, and world-peace advocate Norman Cousins, who told her that "you would be the most pragmatic candidate because you know the direction of the future." He also told her that she was the most pragmatic person he knew, "at the next stage of evolution!"

Once more, Barbara chose not to run. She felt that she lacked a team of peers, ideological partners in the venture that could help keep the campaign out of the political fray and within the loftier framework of a vibrant exchange of ideas. She was looking for "transformationalists, people in tune with the pulse of evolution, who would unify and restore the earth and liberate human creativity," as she put it. In the political arena, such persons were very hard to find. Barbara put away her running shoes—and Ronald Reagan became President.

Finally—an Approach That Made Sense

But now, on a winter evening in 1983, it was being suggested seriously for the third time that she seek a position in the White House. This time it was a wealthy real-estate developer, a man deeply interested in studying higher consciousness, who brought the subject up.

Visiting Barbara at Greystone, the Washington home of her sister (who, you may recall, had been letting Barbara use the house as if it were exclusively hers for years while undertaking a major social-change project), the developer asked her why she didn't use the upcoming '84 political campaign to get her message out.

(Barbara's "message" had remained the same for many years: humanity's evolutionary tale; the need to connect what is working; to encourage people to form small groups to co-create; that everyone's creative talent is needed; that our crises are evolutionary drivers; that humanity is being born as a more co-evolutionary, co-creative species; that when we connect heart with heart, innovation with innovation, we will find that we are being "born" as a universal species in a universe undoubtedly filled with life. She said that we need a "meta-innovation"—one that empowers, connects, and communicates many innovations seen together as elements of a better world, a more peaceful, just, and evolvable world. The Peace Room and the Office for the Future are vital to the next stage of democracy.)

The real-estate magnate Ward Phillips, said: "Why don't you do the one thing that could really make a difference? Take these ideas into the political arena. This is the place where your story can be most effective."

He told her that if she ran, he would back her all the way. (This meant, of course, considerable financial support.)

"You wouldn't be running for President to win," he explained. "You'd be running on principle and to 'tell the story.' There is no one in the world who can do what you can. This story of what this country can do and be could affect civilization forever."

For the third time in as many election cycles, Barbara seriously explored the idea with many friends. One of them, a member of the Democratic Party political establishment in California, offered an alternative that Barbara hadn't before considered.

And that's when it all began.

The Door Is Opened

"I think you should run for the *second* highest office," Jack Baldwin, a political friend, said. "This is, after all, the 'year of the woman' for Vice President. I'm certain that Geraldine Ferraro is going to be nominated to run with Mondale (Walter Mondale, then the presumptive Democratic candidate for President). There couldn't be a better time in party history for your name—the name of another woman—to be placed before the Convention."

Now this seemed real. This seemed doable. This seemed acceptable even to the political establishment. Mondale and the party *were* looking for a female running mate. It was a year to be bold. It was 1984, also the year of Big Brother, as described in the George Orwell novel. She could be an ideal candidate in the great American tradition.

Barbara was in. A long-standing love of the United States, of the evolution of democracy itself, took hold. She was fueled by a sense of "mission" that she had always had, now finding yet another outlet through which to express her ideas.

She announced her decision privately at first, to a group of friends and colleagues at the birthday party of a mutual acquaintance, then made a formal public announcement in Lawrence, Kansas (chosen because it was the fictional site of a significant movie at the time: *The Day After,* which portrayed the world following a nuclear holocaust). Willis Harman of the Stanford Research Institute; Virginia Satir, the great family therapist; and other leaders of the transformational movement were there. She was beginning to amass a major support system.

Barbara's statement began with her opening articulation of a Campaign for a Positive Future, a proposal to "change the game" by pointing to the new reality of "an interdependent world in the nuclear age."

This appeared to be, in fact, exactly what the real-estate developer had promised that a race for high national office could be: a podium from which Barbara could express her most ardently held and socially advanced ideas to a national audience at last. And she was not at a loss for words. . . .

"We are the children of the discontent of the whole world," she said the night at the birthday party when she revealed her intention to run. "We are made up of the people of all cultures who are attracted to the future. The roots of our vision go back to the ancient knowledge of the human race. Our founding fathers gave us a dream that is not the dream of a nation, but the combined aspiration of the peoples of the world."

It was impossible not to get excited when this woman spoke. It was impossible not to be inspired.

"We will build a platform for the future, beyond liberal or conservative," she would say. "We are launching a campaign for the future in every field. There are examples of solutions and innovations in environment, health, education, defense, economics . . . every way in which we endeavor. We will take these examples and form a pragmatic synthesis of What Works.

"We are not facing a missile gap, but a *vision* gap. That's the gap we commit to fill!"

People were on their feet.

The Media's Illness

Alas, the Establishment was not.

And the media, long a part of that Establishment, led the way in ignoring vice presidential candidate Barbara Marx Hubbard. For one thing, her message was too positive. As far as the printed press and every major national electronic outlet were concerned, if a thing wasn't negative, the thing wasn't news.

In that interview with Jeffrey Mishlove years later, Barbara would articulate this perfectly. . . .

MISHLOVE: . . . So many people feel nihilistic, pessimistic. They don't have a positive vision. In fact, the old vision is often one of Armageddon, one of tragedy, one of heat death. There are many negative images.

BARBARA: Yes, there are, and partly I think mass media has a disease. I call it *disempathitis* of the nervous system—dead on empathy.

If you think of the media as our collective nervous system, it's filtering out good news. If something creative, innovative, or loving happens, that's not news. But if something is burned, killed, or destroyed, *that* is news.

So we are being constantly flooded with information of our breakdown, but not concurrently and equally with our innovations, our loving. So we have a very bad self-image. The media is giving us a nervous breakdown. . . .

MISHLOVE: There's a kind of cultural cynicism that's so common.

BARBARA: I feel that if the news were interpreted as the news of what is growing, what is evolving, you would find a new situation very rapidly. The way I ran for Vice President was that I proposed a Peace Room as sophisticated as the War Room in the White House, to map every innovation and success—to connect it and to communicate it live over television, on a continuous basis—until we could see the emerging world. And a person like me seeks out the emerging world. . . .

The media is overlooking the story of our birth. Think about a baby's nervous system—when a baby is crying, the nervous system puts the baby to sleep. Our mass media puts us to sleep. . . . Maybe we have to feel more pain before we can truly wake up.

(The above is excerpted from the "Planetary Birth" episode of the *Thinking Allowed* television series. See **www.thinkingallowed .com/2bhubbard.html**.)

A Political Miracle

Barbara pulled off the impossible in her vice presidential campaign. She made her way to the Democratic National Convention in San Francisco with no money, no media, and no passes to the floor. She knew the wife of the governor of Colorado, and she and members of her volunteer team managed to get in. She spoke to morning caucus after morning caucus of convention delegates, hoping to gather commitments. She needed 200 delegates to get her name placed in nomination from the floor. It seemed impossible.

Barbara was gathering some steam behind her, however. Some 90 Positive Future Centers had formed around her campaign all across the country. They originally had been created when Barbara asked Carolyn Anderson and her husband, Sanford Anderson, to be the campaign managers. Carolyn lived in Palo Alto and was gifted at building resonance and small groups. The campaign itself was launched at her home. She invited the 12 most outstanding, socially sophisticated, transformationally oriented people she knew to join together in a powerful "fire ceremony," committing their lives, their fortunes, and their sacred honor to bringing this campaign, and its purpose, into the American political scene.

The Positive Future Centers established a "telethon." All were linked by telephone, creating a resonant field of these small groups, which were dedicated to the "impossible dream" of a little known futurist who was entering a Democratic Convention cold, trying to get the required 200 delegates . . . while many famous politicians were also trying, often just for a chance to address the nation. She was told she would be "lucky to get one delegate, if it were your mother!"

The small team of supporters who prepared to go to the convention decided to practice every metaphysical teaching they had ever learned. They were all reading *A Course in Miracles* and were forgiving and loving everyone. Most important, they practiced "structural tension."

In this process, you choose a goal or vision, and then if doubt comes in, don't deny it, simply re-choose it, again and again. When you do so consistently, no matter how much doubt floods you, the higher choice creates a structural tension. Eventually, like a rubber band, the doubts spring up to meet the goal, and it becomes a reality.

That said, Barbara well knew that her task was gargantuan. She had graduated from Bryn Mawr College cum laude in political science. She was no dummy. Yet because her guidance was so strong and her vision so clear, and because the support of thousands of local groups resonating with their own passion to create joined in a single focus, the "rubber band snapped." The vision began to materialize, even though few delegates had ever heard of Barbara Marx Hubbard. Many of those who knew who she was considered her part of the "human potential movement," which they had very little respect for and zero political loyalty.

Barbara had to beg to even be given a time slot at those morning caucuses: "Please! Thirty seconds. Just give me 30 seconds."

The people who controlled who got to "pitch" convention delegates could hardly say no. It was, after all, a national convention of the *Democratic* Party. What basis could they use to deny her just a half minute of time in front of the room?

Each state's caucus made sure to put her on first—sometimes as early as 6 o'clock in the morning—when whatever delegates who even made it to the caucus room on time were bleary-eyed.

She learned to cram her message into a half-minute pitch:

"My name is Barbara Marx Hubbard. I ask you to place my name in nomination for the vice presidency so I can propose an Office for the Future and a Peace Room in the White House under the direction of the vice president, which will track innovations, breakthroughs, and projects that work so that we can strategize victories over hunger, disease, injustice, and war; and so we can find out what is working in America and the world."

It worked.

It actually worked.

She spoke with an authenticity that in 30 seconds made the obvious benefit of her ideas undeniably apparent. She wound up with *more than the 200 delegates* required, all committed to supporting her nomination on the convention floor.

The political "professionals" behind the scenes were flummoxed and didn't know what to do. Geraldine Ferraro was Walter Mondale's choice for a running mate. Everyone understood that going in. Where did this *Hubbard woman* come from? *And what is she trying to prove?*

Totally blindsided, the backroom boys scrambled. I can hear the heated discussions even now. "We can invalidate her delegates!" someone must surely have suggested. "She needs 200 valid signatures. We can find something 'wrong' with just enough to get her under the number."

"No, no," another, wiser voice probably inserted. "She's got more than 200. We'll never convince anybody that over *one-third* of the signatures are invalid. She's got a whole contingency out there now."

"Yeah, well, you got a better idea?"

"Get her in here. *Talk to her.* Tell her she doesn't have a chance in the world on a national ticket with Walter Mondale. A woman with no political background whatsoever? It will never happen. She'll take down the entire ticket. *Tell her that!* Tell her that if she'll turn her committed delegates over to Ferraro, we'll make sure she gets her name placed in nomination. She'll make history. And she'll get to make her speech to the floor. That's all her people want anyway."

"What's she talking about?"

"Something about a 'Peace Room' in the White House under the direction of the vice president. Something about an 'Office for the Future.' And don't roll your eyes. *She's getting delegates.*"

"All right. Somebody talk to her, and tell her that if she'll stand down and make room for Ferraro, we'll make room for her to stand up for her ideas."

I just made that whole dialogue up. But you know what? I bet I've come very close to some of the things that were said. Because guess what? That's exactly what happened.

It was announced that two women's names would be placed in nomination for vice president: Geraldine Ferraro and Barbara Marx Hubbard. It was a shock to the whole Hubbard support group. They weren't even at the Convention Center!

The Party officials moved the agenda forward and told her that she was going to speak a few hours earlier. Barbara knew what this was about. Her new time slot was before national television coverage kicked in. They were trying to hide her. She was, however, officially *on*. Her group drove like mad from Marin, where they had been staying. She was writing the speech in the car. With all the visioning, it hadn't really seemed possible. Yet it was. She titled the speech "To Fulfill the Dream."

As she was led up to the giant podium, a guard took her arm. "Now, honey," he said, "they won't pay any attention to you. They never do. You're saying this to the Universe!" And so she did.

In her fundamental theme, she enlarged the vision of Thomas Jefferson:

> We hold these truths to be self-evident,
> All people are born creative
> Endowed by our creator with the unalienable
>   right and responsibility
> To express our creativity
> For the good of our selves, our families, and the
>   whole community.

The Ideas She Stood Up For

Barbara Marx Hubbard came, in political terms, "out of nowhere" to have her name placed in nomination for vice president of the United States at the national convention of one of America's two dominant political parties. She gave her speech from the Big Podium before the convention.

Do you know how many people get to speak from the Big Podium as a vice presidential candidate at a major party's political convention? Do you know how many *women* get to do so? Do you know how many women got to do so 25 years ago? Do you know how tightly that particular time slot is controlled?

Many people around the country (including some of Barbara's own family and the few of her friends who doubted) must have thought that her campaign was quixotic, at best—and must then have sat back in stunned amazement as she stood before an every-four-year gathering of some of the nation's most powerful political operatives to share her sparkling ideas about how to create a remarkable future.

And what kinds of ideas did Barbara advance? The same things she had been saying throughout her campaign—when the media wouldn't listen.

"I come before you today to propose a New Social Function," Barbara had been declaring for months. "One that can liberate human creativity, moving us toward a new process *of* the Whole, *by* the Whole, *for* the Whole. This new function will be guided in the Office of the Future and the Peace Room, under the supervision of the vice president of the United States, in the White House.

"The Peace Room will eventually become as sophisticated as the War Room, where we are now kept busy tracking every possible danger and strategizing how to defeat it.

"In our Peace Room, we will track every innovation, solution, and breakthrough. We will look at every idea being tried everywhere to see What Works. We will map how to get from where we are to where we choose to go. And we will *share* what we learn with all who choose to join us in working toward one common goal: a sustainable and bountiful future for life on Earth.

"I will propose such Peace Rooms in every other country with which we have diplomatic ties. These will be places where that which is rising in our society can converge, cooperate, and be empowered. In the Peace Room, we will strategize our victories over our common enemies of hunger, disease, injustice, and war itself. In the Peace Rooms, *we will change the world.*"

To Barbara it seemed clear: the new political expression would be *holism*. She wrote in her journal at the time: "We are at the beginning of the age of the whole. We are becoming an interdependent world. What is being born is the idea of holism. The whole person, the whole community, the whole world. What 'freedom' was to the 18th century, 'holism' is to the 20th. It's a new concept. When it achieves its political expression, it will be as big a step forward as the institutionalization of freedom."

These are the remarkable thoughts of this remarkable woman at a remarkable time in humanity's history.

Was It All Worth It?

Had the months-long, energy-draining effort produced all that Barbara hoped it would? No. The Mondale/Ferraro ticket didn't seem too interested in publicly (or privately) proposing a Peace Room or an Office for the Future in the White House. And a few months later, the ticket lost the election anyway.

Had the effort produced any worthwhile outcomes at all? Yes. The message of social change, collaborative creation, and consciousness awakening had been heard by many more people than ever before. The notoriety alone that Barbara gained from having her name placed in nomination for the second-highest political office in America brought thousands of new readers to her books, hundreds of new attendees to her lectures, and dozens of devoted new volunteers all over the country waiting and wanting to help her put her ideas into motion.

The most unexpected aspect of the campaign, the spontaneous formation of those Positive Future Centers around the country, was important. "The inner work of personal growth and the outer work of social action was combined in their workings," Barbara said when looking back, and they marked "the emergence of a new social form—a unit that was transforming its members from self-centered to whole-centered consciousness and action."

This, of course, has been Barbara's life goal from the beginning. For more than 30 years, she has been championing the creation of "a new social architecture" that might change the world. And while the Positive Future Centers inspired by her vice presidential bid all but disappeared when the campaign was over, the impulse had been felt, the seed had been planted, and a new idea arose among many thousands of people of the role that they themselves could play in the forward movement of their own species and the co-creation of their future.

As Barbara put it in retrospect: "The effect of the campaign was not on the current political reality, but on those of us who fought for it. We know that a small group can perform political miracles if its members align on a vision and give it their all."

No Next Step

After a period of natural letdown following the hectic political campaign (which she later called the "adventure of my life," taking her to one city after another for many months), Barbara had no idea what she was going to do next. It disappointed her that she didn't know how to keep the Positive Future Centers alive. There were many who tried to help, yet the organizational structure and financials were not there. She was in debt. She had to spend several years lecturing and teaching for fees in order to pay back what she owed. *What's next?* she asked herself over and over again.

One day she had gone to her favorite monastery, Mt. Calvary, in Santa Barbara. Rising at dawn, she was sitting in the beautiful garden as the sun rose over the clay roofs, the hummingbirds fluttering near her. She wrote in her journal: "Create an aura of silence about you till you can hear me at all times. When the hour of our birth is at hand, everyone will be called to their posts." The inner work began.

Yet she continued with her social mission. Her friend Rama Vernon, one of the great yoga teachers in the United States, came to her, saying, "Barbara, you will find your destiny in the Soviet Union. I want you to lead a group there to overcome fear and make new relationships."

Barbara said *yes*. She became one of many citizen diplomats leading hundreds of Americans to the Soviet Union just before perestroika and glasnost—a delegation engaging in small group discussions and informal visits between the Soviet and American people.

The idea was to work from the ground up in improving relations between the two nations, and Barbara had been invited by the Center for Soviet-American Dialogue, which had arranged the trip in conjunction with the Soviet Peace Committee in the Soviet Union. It turned out to be the first of several such journeys that she would make over the next few years as both Russian and American citizens made their visits back and forth.

Yet even with all this, Barbara felt incomplete, unsettled—and unaccomplished. Her "lost years" had begun. She couldn't seem to

get any particular outreach or project completely unwound, operating with financial stability, and producing long-term results on
the ground.

She was beginning to lose motivation. She'd found a small
house to rent in Irvine, California, which she shared with friends
from the campaign who wanted to go forward with her in her
work. But she was really drifting in an interior wilderness without
a home, her children grown, and her life companion lost to an
untimely death. . . .

22.

*EPISODE #10: LOSING A COMPANION,
THE VERY END OF 1981: Two Years Before
the Vice Presidential Campaign . . .*

The beautiful strains of "Silent Night," played by an orchestra of mostly strings and accompanied by an angelic choir, fills the air.

Someone must have a radio on, very quietly, in another room. Or perhaps it is the hospital's own overhead speaker system.

John Whiteside is the second long-term relationship of Barbara's life. She is sitting by his hospital bed now, holding his hand, watching him closely.

It is Christmas Eve, and the man with whom Barbara had developed SYNCONS; the man with whom she had created the Theater for the Future (the very basis for the Day One event over 30 years later); the man who has given her emotional, administrative, logistical, and even production support for just about every idea she ever had over the past dozen years . . . her life companion and lover is living his final moments.

It is lung cancer.

The man smoked three packs of cigarettes a day. When the prognosis came, 20 months earlier, he wouldn't believe it and didn't accept it. But as time passed, it became clear: he only had a short time left.

Barbara nursed him through his last months at Greystone, where they'd lived for over a decade. One day he was lying in bed, smiling.

"What are you smiling about?" Barbara asked, feeling deeply deserted and sad at the thought of losing his life, his partnership, his friendship.

John answered: "Sunshine, I know you will do it. Mankind will be born into the Universe, and you will do your part."

He must have felt at some deep level that he had done what he could on this Earth. The need to make the work the two were doing together financially viable was taxing and almost impossible. He didn't want to fail, yet the structures of modern society weren't able to support it.

Now, on Christmas Eve, Barbara leaves the hospital for the night, exhausted, making plans to return early in the morning. John was neither moving nor talking. A tiny, emaciated version of himself, he simply lay in bed in a fetal position. He dies not long after she leaves.

She cries after getting the call, but there's nothing she can do at the hospital. The nurse on the phone gently suggests that she try to get a little sleep and come first thing in the morning. Barbara makes an effort, between heaving sobs, but she gets only a few minutes here and there. Finally, restless, she rises before dawn and returns to the hospital.

Barbara had never seen a dead body. She observed later that it was as unbelievable as birth. *Where are you?* she wonders now. When she touches him, she is momentarily taken aback to find his body hardening and cold.

Standing by his bed, tears blur her sight.

"Oh, John . . . John. . . ." The words escape her in a whispered cry. "Why did you die?"

She is startled to hear his reply in a voice so clear she would have sworn he was right there (which, of course, he was).

I died to set you free. I have work to do to prepare for what is coming. We will rendezvous again.

"Where have you gone?" she begs him to tell her.

To create the big SYNCON in the sky! There seems to be almost a smile in his voice at the little joke he's made. Then . . .

I will be ready when you need me.

And that was it.

He says, in his old Air Force way: *Over and out.*

How It Began

Barbara and John met in the fall of 1969: she a housewife and mother of five living in the New York suburb of Lakeville, Connecticut; he an Air Force lieutenant colonel stationed in New York City as a media rep. Their relationship was an outgrowth of her passion for telling what she called a "New Story" about humanity's future and of her idea that America's space program was an important part of that story.

Their early acquaintanceship grew into a friendship, which evolved into a deeply meaningful relationship. (More about that will come later, because it changed the direction of her whole life. Not just what she did, but *who she was.*)

Barbara called John every day during one of the most significant periods of her life—a time in February 1980, ten years into their partnership—when she encountered, during several months away from him to write a book, the second astonishing spiritual encounter of her life . . . an awakening she always referred to thereafter as "The Christ Experience."

She could not have known that even as she was being filled with more energy and inspiration than ever before, John's own energy was beginning to slip away.

He told her so when she returned, overflowing with excitement after completing her work on the book. When John heard her first description of the Christ Experience over the telephone weeks earlier, just after it occurred, he was taken aback.

"Barbara . . ." was all he could say for a moment. "Barbara . . ." Then he collected himself. "I'm amazed. This is profoundly amazing."

"Yes, but what do you think of it?" Barbara asked from the other end of the line.

John didn't hesitate for a moment. "I would stake my life on the truth of it."

Now Barbara was home at Greystone showing him her manuscript. It was thick. Very thick. "What are you calling it?" he asked her.

"*The Book of Co-Creation*. It's all there—everything."

John flipped its pages. "My God, it's the Bible, rewritten!" he gasped.

"Well, not quite." Barbara chuckled. "Just the New Testament . . ."

"Oh, *just* the New Testament." He laughed with her.

Finding Out—and Not Believing

A few weeks later, at dinner in New York, John seemed distracted, unfocused.

"John?"

Barbara said it as a question, and the single word carried the fullness of her concern. And so he looked at her now . . . deciding. Then his shoulders dropped, along with his voice.

"Something's wrong with me, Barbara, and I don't know what it is."

She watched an emotion etch itself on his face—a look she'd never seen before. It wasn't concern, and it wasn't frustration or annoyance. If she had to give it a name, she would have said *fear,* yet she knew that was completely out of character for this man. Perhaps *mystified apprehension* might have been a better label.

John noticed her noticing him, and he quickly and correctly assessed that, as usual, he was hiding nothing from her. She was aware, and he could see she was aware, that for the first time since the day they met, he was not "on top of" what was going on. So he decided to tell her everything.

"I'm depressed. I've lost my energy, my drive," he said. "And . . ."

He paused. *Should* he worry her? Should he tell her?

"What, John? *'And'* what?"

"And . . . there's this pain in my chest."

Now it was Barbara's turn to pause. Then, softly: "Darling, what does the doctor say?"

"I haven't seen a doctor."

"You haven't seen a doctor? John, you have got to have a checkup."

"I know. I mean, I suppose I should—"

"There's no 'supposing,' John. You're going."

The soldier had received his marching orders, and he knew better than to ignore his "commanding officer." He went.

The doctor found a lesion—the result, he guessed, of John's years as a coal miner. The pain grew worse. Then Barbara noticed one day that John was having trouble buttoning the cuff of his shirt.

"Here, let me do that," she offered, and he did, but not without a strained expression crossing his face. Barbara knew he couldn't have liked to be helped with a simple thing that he should have been able to do for himself. "John?" she asked, once more posing her one-word question.

He caught her eye and squinted just a bit, cocking his head as he'd done so many, many times. He had this way of locking eyes with her almost instantly when something joyful, fun, exciting, stimulating, inspiring, or . . . sexual . . . was on his mind.

This time it was none of that.

"I can't seem to get my hands to work right," he muttered. "I can't button my cuffs, I can't close my collar . . ."

"Oh, John—"

"And the pain has moved to my back."

"My God, John, how long—" She interrupted herself. "It doesn't matter. We need to go back to the doctor right away."

The second diagnosis was more definitive, and the doctor was direct. Barbara remembers just a string of phrases: "Lung cancer . . . metastasized to the brain . . . a few months to live . . . get your affairs in order . . ."

The silence in the car on the way back to Greystone was itself deadening. Then abruptly, John blurted, "I don't accept that, and

I don't believe it!" His hand banged the steering wheel. "I'll have this beat before Christmas."

At the house, he opened a window to catch the June air, lit his third cigarette since leaving the doctor's office, and poured himself a drink.

Six Months Later

The beautiful strains of "Silent Night," played by an orchestra of mostly strings and accompanied by an angelic choir, fills the air.

Someone must have a radio on, very quietly, in another room. Or perhaps it is the hospital's own overhead speaker system. . . .

♪ ♪ ♪

23.

EPISODE #9: THE CHRIST EXPERIENCE, 1980—
Two Years Prior to Losing a Companion . . .

I've now said a couple of times that Barbara's life has revolved around three remarkable spiritual encounters in her 80-plus years. The third one—and most recent to the writing of this book—we have chosen to call The Contact. It occurred in 2002, and you've already read about it. We've called the first episode The Birth Revelation, which occurred in 1966; you'll read about it a bit later on as we continue to step backward into Barbara's story. This leaves The Christ Experience—which is every bit as amazing as the other two, and every bit as important in helping us understand the formative factors in Barbara Marx Hubbard's life.

In fact, this is so crucial that I've decided *not* to write about it. The experience is so subjective, so singular and personal, that *no one can tell it better than Barbara*. So I'm going to let her do it. I'm simply going to pull out all the notes, resources, and prior manuscripts that she has placed at my disposal and allow Barbara herself to describe the experience in her own words.

Beyond the fact that no one can tell it better than she can, there's another reason I want Barbara's words to replace any of my own in this next section. What Barbara took from what she refers to as her Christ Experience is a teaching, a message, and a revelation that I believe needs to be placed in this book *exactly as it was received*—without me attempting to interpolate, translate, or report on anything.

So I'm now going to bow out as a writer and turn you over to Barbara's collected notes—with this exception: I dropped in a few subheads to break up the type a little.

Here, then, is Barbara's own description of The Christ Experience, followed by the revelation she received about What It All Means. . . .

In Barbara's Own Words, Gathered from Her Notes and Journals . . .

It was 1980. I had turned 50, during menopause.

One day when I was down in the basement at Greystone cleaning, I heard an inner voice: *Barbara, would you like to die?* I was startled. The voice was tempting, seductive. *Well,* I thought, *it might be nice . . . but I'm not finished yet.*

The voice continued: *Would you like to get cancer, or would you like to rejuvenate? Cancer is the body's panicked effort to grow without a plan. Rejuvenation happens when you discover the deeper plan for your life and say yes.*

I pondered that, nodded to the voice, and said to myself: *I choose to rejuvenate. I choose to discover the deeper plan for my life. . . .*

I realized that when we stop giving birth to children, we are ready to give birth to ourselves.

Saying *yes* to the "plan" is welcoming the birth of the self. For the feminine co-creator, this is the next stage of her life. It is open-ended. We don't yet know where it will lead. Since I'd decided to go the whole way in this lifetime, I knew that saying *yes* to this voice would reveal my greater destiny.

I was planning to do a book that was to focus on the future of humanity [now available as *The Evolutionary Journey*]. I knew I couldn't do it at Greystone, where there was way too much going on. I said to John: "I've got to get out of Washington and find a quiet place to write." I rented a small house in Santa Barbara for three months and went out there, calling John every day to let him know how the writing was going.

The news was not good. The writing was not "going" at all. In fact, I had a bad case of writer's block. One day I just gave up and invited my sister Jacqueline to come visit me. I figured that I just needed to get my mind off of it completely for a while. She flew down from Stanford, where her husband taught law at the university.

I had been asking the Universe a question: "What kind of person can handle all this new power that humans have?" I could see that if we used all of our new powers well, we would completely transcend the current human condition—even the animal-human life cycle itself.

Just as we have no image of our collective future, I realized we have no positive images of ourselves in that future. We are not going to become Jesus Christ or the Buddha. Futurists offered images of bionic women, high-tech monsters, and space beings. . . . *Who are we becoming?*

It was more than Maslow's self-actualizing human. Humans are being born into the new culture of high technology with the power of gods; this new phase of human being has the potential to change all of life.

But who has seen the glory of what we can become so we can aim at it? This was my question.

With this question, and the frustration of my writer's block, I drove with my sister through the gorgeous, shining hills of Santa Barbara. It was February, and the weather in Southern California was perfect.

We got lost. I saw a little sign that said: MT. CALVARY MONASTERY.

I had a sudden déjà vu experience and said to my sister, "Jacqueline, I've been here before!" Tears came into my eyes. A sense of great expectancy gripped me as we drove up the winding road.

Awareness on the Mountain

We came to a little monastery overlooking the mountains and sea. For some reason, I suddenly looked up and there, magically, appeared humanlike butterflies, afloat past the cross in my view in an ecstasy of joy and freedom!

It turns out there was a hang gliders' club jumping off a higher mountain, about 50 people in wings above Mount Calvary. In a blinding flash, an idea filled my mind: Mass metamorphosis. We shall all be changed. We *are* all *being* changed.

Then I had an inner experience of the Christ—not just as Jesus of Nazareth; but as an omniscient, omnipresent Essence that was actually pulling us forward toward the total and radical fulfillment of our Divine human potential. And I heard the words . . .

My resurrection was real. It is a forecast of what the human race will do collectively when you love God above all else, your neighbor as yourself, and yourself as a godlike being, combined with science and technology. You will all be changed.

I thought: *Oh my God, Western civilization was built on a story of the radical transformation of the person to life everlasting. Believing that we would be changed, we developed the technologies to actually change ourselves. Through science, democracy, technology, and industry, we're learning to extend our life span. We're learning to build new body parts. We're learning to live in outer space. But we forgot that the image of who we are becoming is that of a Christlike being. Not Jesus Christ, but co-creators.*

One more electrifying idea flashed through my mind: *This is why we are given the power of gods. It is to radically and totally transform ourselves into co-creative beings on a universal scale.*

I was filled with awareness that our high technology is dangerous in a closed-system Earth with self-conscious humans fighting and polluting, but they may be *natural capacities* of a universal species when the time comes. We are practicing now for our future life, both on this Earth and in space, when we will shift to the next stage of our evolution as a universal species. *Jesus was the prototype of the future human.*

The planetary birth is actually the moment for this kind of human to come forth on Earth *en masse* for the first time. Women are leading the way. This is the deeper meaning of the feminine co-creator.

The Revelations Continue

I checked into the monastery for a silent retreat the next week and began to hear a Christlike voice. I "received" a stream of words in this way. . . .

> *You, all of you who are desirous and ready, are the Way. Be a beacon of light unto yourselves. This tiny band—this brave congregation of souls attracted to the future of the world—is my avant-garde. These are self-selected souls who are here to carry the miracle of the Resurrection into action as the transformation of humanity from Homo sapiens to Homo Universalis.*
>
> *Oh, humanity, what your eyes are about to behold will fill your breaking heart with joy.*
>
> *You who is saddened by the infantile condition of the human race take heed. Lift up your heart, raise your eyes, throw back your head, and sing praises for the day that is coming. . . .*

The voice continued every day. I returned to the New Testament and experienced it as coded evolution. When we read it from the perspective of what we are becoming, we can see that the story of Jesus prefigured our own future. The virgin birth, the miracles, the death of this body, the emergence of a new body sensitive to thought—is this not what may be possible as we put together our full capacities?

Only from the vantage point of the evolutionary future can we fully understand the code of the scriptures. It is not metaphysical, allegorical, mystical, or alone. It is evolutionary.

That means the change will occur to us in real time, in history, just as it is said that the life of Christ occurred in history. That's the point. The whole story may be *coming true* through *us* as we enter the period of *conscious evolution*.

Writer's Block Ends

I went through the Gospels, Acts, Epistles, and the book of Revelation, verse by verse, writing for six months without stopping or "thinking" in the ordinary sense. I just asked "What does this mean?" and the ideas flowed through a poised mind. It was the most wonderful period of my life. I produced a massive treatise that was called *The Book of Co-Creation*.

[The last section, inspired by the book of Revelation, has been published as *The Revelation: A Message of Hope for the New Millennium*.]

I was infused with the spirit of the evolutionary Christ and felt that this is what we can become, as we are all being changed.

The Magic of <u>Yes</u> . . .

There were two basic commandments I received. The first was: *Be Me . . . all of you. I want demonstrations now, Barbara.*

I replied: "I choose it, but I don't know how to do it."

The response was: *Did you know how to be born? Did you know how to do puberty? You choose it; I will do it.*

I chose it, just like I had said *yes* to the question of rejuvenation. All of these *yes* responses began to affect my very DNA, I believe. This is the deepest meaning of *self-evolution*. We evolve our selves when we say *yes* to our dormant potential and act upon it. Each *yes* unlocks one more code.

The second key revelation was: the alternative to Armageddon is a planetary Pentecost. It will be a time when a critical mass of people will hear from within—in their own voices and languages —the inner words of God.

I saw that this was an early preparation for the potential of the planetary birth experience, which is a generic, inclusive version of the same pre-inspired experience. I was told that we should work together for the *planetary* Pentecost in our lifetime, not as a religion, but as an experience of an evolving humanity such that we could all hear our own inner voices in our own languages. It would be the voice of Spirit heard by a critical mass of humanity from within each person, thereby evolving ourselves and changing the world.

We should form "evolutionary circles" of two or more, to birth ourselves as Universal Humans. For in that field of resonance, we shall all be changed.

The church of the future is the person evolved. The fulfillment of the Judeo-Christian story is the story of each of us becoming co-creators with the Divine.

I had heard the words: *Do not abandon my church—evolve it. Expand my church into a new vehicle for the new beings and the resurrection of the body politic.*

What is "the resurrection of the body politic" but the radical transformation of all our systems, applying our new technologies and capacities to be in alignment with nature and Spirit?

When we combine the full range of our scientific and social potential with our emerging spirituality, we shall see ourselves revealed. *This is the meaning of our new powers*—a question I had asked so many years before.

I began to catch a glimpse of ourselves in the future as Universal Humans, connected through the heart to the whole of life, guiding new technologies to restore the earth, free the people, and explore the Universe within and beyond. I was totally, deeply excited. The hormonal energy of transformation was activating my very cells. It was, in truth, a form of rejuvenation.

Every day, I called John from Santa Barbara to read to him what I wrote.

I shared my thesis that during the transition (which we entered in 1945, when we gained new power to destroy or co-create), the veil is thinning. The soul is incarnating and preparing individuals for self-evolution, leading to "resurrection"—that is, transformation and actual transubstantiation, or metamorphosis, divinization of the body, or a universal embodied Self. As an old soldier and Southern Baptist, John was astonished. And he loved it. He told me he would stake his life on the truth of it.

(THE END OF BARBARA'S NOTES, WRITINGS, AND
JOURNAL ENTRIES ON THE CHRIST EXPERIENCE)

✣

I want to acknowledge here that it is daring and courageous of Barbara to have allowed me to publish many excerpts from the private journal entries she gave me, originally, as background and research material for this book. Without such access, we would never know what spiritual queries and mystical insights have fueled the engine of her experience. We would have learned much about the exterior, but nothing about the interior, of her life. Yet it is in the interior of a person's life where the real treasure lies, where the meaning resides, where the richness is—and where the real opportunity for learning is for all of us.

For instance, Barbara writes in her journal that she has experienced Christ as "actually pulling us forward toward the total and radical fulfillment of our Divine human potential." We may agree or disagree with that interpretation of His life, but I must share it with you if I'm to tell you Barbara's story Complete. And so I thank Barbara for her giving us permission to see her in total transparency.

Barbara Marx Hubbard's whole life had led to the three spiritual encounters that have marked her journey: The Birth Revelation, The Christ Experience, and The Contact. Had her life not been uniquely designed to both motivate her and *allow* her to spend years searching for, and then telling, the story of humanity's present reality, those three spiritual encounters *might have been mistaken* by Barbara as simply *disconnected and meaningless images* even as they were flashing before her.

The fact that she was *prepared* for those images—that they made sense to her even as they were arriving—is what gave them their impact.

And were it not for those spiritual encounters, her life would likely have *never culminated in the Day One event* of 2012—which all of *us* now have an opportunity to join in co-creating, inasmuch as *we* have had our encounter *with this book*.

Do you see how it all works?

🍃 🍃 🍃

REFLECTIONS & EXPLORATIONS

Clarity and Vision Belong to All of Us

As we reflect on the times just described, and look more closely at Barbara's experience to see what we all might benefit from, we are reminded that . . .

> . . . mystical experiences are Life's gift to all of us.
> There is not a single one of us who has not had them;
> there is not a single one of them that is meaningless; and,
> like snowflakes, there are no two that are exactly alike.

We may call our experiences something else, we may not recognize them for what they are when they occur, or we may write them off as figments of our imagination, but all of us are being gifted by Life itself with communications *from* Life itself, in many forms.

Barbara called her 1980 encounter a "Christ Experience." That labeling was, perhaps, a product of her Western culture, of the particular environment in which she had her encounter (she was, after all, at a Catholic monastery), of her own identification of Jesus Christ as both a spiritual *revolutionary* and a spiritual *evolutionary,* or of some other factor unknown and not considered here. It doesn't matter.

Whatever it's called, the moment is essentially the same for everyone: an opening to peace, wisdom, clarity, and love that transcends normal human experience; a filling up with thoughts never heretofore occurring to us; an expansion of awareness beyond all previous limits. And often, a glimpse or a vision of a future beyond most people's imagining—such that one might be better off not to speak of it to others unless one is prepared to be looked at askance.

Barbara has been looked at askance, at least by some, for half a century. For she has been receiving guidance from what she has described variously as an "inner voice" long before her Christ Experience, and long before her experience of "Contact" in August of 2002. And, right along, she has been sharing with others all the glimpses of a Future Possible that she has gleaned from those moments.

Yet while some have wrinkled their brows and wondered aloud what Barbara is talking about, others have found her to be prescient. Buckminster Fuller called her "the best informed human now alive regarding Futurism." Jonas Salk said that she was one of the few people in the world who completely understood his far-reaching visions for tomorrow. And she has stopped powerful people—such as President Eisenhower—in their tracks with her questions, while leaving other people of influence—such as Abraham Maslow, Thomas Merton, Lewis Mumford, among them—deeply impressed, even if they didn't totally concur with all of her thinking and insights.

Of course, clarity and vision are accessible by all of us. That's the point here. That's the reason for writing this book. Barbara Marx Hubbard is just an ordinary person. She's been married and divorced, she has birthed and raised five children, she's had out-of-wedlock lovers, and she's had multiple life callings and several "minicareers." True, some of her outward adventures have been a step or two removed from the Small Town USA variety, but all of them have fallen within the framework of normal human encounters.

Barbara is not the only person, after all, to have run for vice president. She's not even the only *woman* to do so. Neither is she the only person to have asked a President a question he had no answer for. She is not alone in initiating projects seeking to improve life for humanity as a whole, nor in deeply pondering the innermost matters of the soul.

Nothing that Barbara Marx Hubbard has done sets her so far apart from the rest of us that we can't identify with her—or imagine ourselves being like her. And that's what I hope this book will allow us to do. I hope it will enable all of us to imagine ourselves being *just like Barbara:* hearing the voice of Wisdom and Clarity just like Barbara; experiencing the Divine Within just like Barbara; expressing the essence of Who We Are just like Barbara; and moving from the Essential Self to the Universal Self . . . just like Barbara.

We *can* do this—and thus, change the world. For when we *all* do this, life on Earth cannot possibly remain the same. Yet in *order* to do this, we will have to let go of many of our previous ideas about who we are, why we are here, and what life is all about. We will have to join the Legion of the Courageous Ones: those who have chosen to make a *life,* rather than a living.

We can begin by asking ourselves when we get up tomorrow morning: *Am I going off today to do things that make my soul sing? Is my activity on this day that which expands my heart, enlivens my mind, and blesses my world?*

If the answer is *no,* ask yourself: *Then why am I doing this?*

I'll always remember what the late Dr. Elisabeth Kübler-Ross (psychiatrist and world-famous author of books on death and dying) said to me when I was in my late 30s. Having met her at a lecture, I told her that I was doing work I hated, so meaningless did I find it.

"Why do you do that?" she asked me.

"I have to, in order to survive."

"You are not surviving," she announced. "You are among the walking dead."

Within a month, I resigned from my job.

To do something like this, we have to know that life's greatest opportunity, the invitation of *conscious evolution,* truly *is* open to all of us. Life itself is constantly extending us this invitation.

We will explore this truth deeply on the pages ahead, through the telling of more and more of Barbara's story.

Enjoy.

24.

EPISODE #8: TELLING THE NEW STORY, 1979—
A Year Before the Christ Experience . . .

It's interesting, isn't it, how we can be doing things "today" in preparation for "tomorrow" and not even know it? Only when we look back over our lives do we realize that so much of what we've done (I want to say *all* of what we've done) has been a "rehearsal" for what is going on right now. . . .

Barbara herself actually created a forerunner of the future Day One event *33 years earlier.* She had been sharing the story of what she conceived of as "humanity's birth" for what seems like most of her adult life—but now, in this final year of the decade, she found an exciting *new* way to do so, and it is just what she needed to keep her own interest up.

That might seem a strange thing to say about somebody unless they're right on top of the half-century mark, have made the same speech, given the same interview, or written the same magazine piece a hundred times or more.

Politicians know. They create what they call a "stump speech" and deliver it wherever they go, with minor variations attuned to location. Ministers know. They preach the same sermons every year, with minor variations attuned to the season. Authors know. They write the same three books over and over again, with a little shift in plot or approach.

Eventually, everyone gets tired of saying the same thing in the same old way, particularly when, after a while, the number of unused variations on the theme begins to diminish.

But now, in 1979, Barbara and John Whiteside have found a new way to say what Barbara has been sharing since she was 36 years old. They've wrapped her message in a piece of *stagecraft*, complete with original music, sound effects, and special lighting. They're calling it:

THE THEATER FOR THE FUTURE
A Preview of Coming Attractions

There is no way that either of them can know that this little production—which they've packed into a huge trunk and are carrying around the country like little-known rock stars—will provide much of the basis for a full-stage spectacular, telecast over the Internet to a worldwide audience some *33 years later*. This is, it turns out, the Mother of All Out-of-Town Tryouts.

Barbara and John have become clear that if the New Story (as Barbara has been calling it since 1966) is not designed in a way that allows people to easily "get it" and *enjoy* getting it, no one is going to get it at all. At least, none but a handful. And Barbara needs more than a handful—she wants the *whole of humanity* to hear this!

The Precursor of the "Day One" Event

And so now, in yet another city in yet another rented venue, the room darkens. Barbara stands in a suddenly appearing pool of light, describing the quest for meaning, then inviting people to see life in a new way.

"Imagine the universe, billions and billions of galaxies, multitudes of solar systems . . . some may have life comparable to our own," she begins.

She then takes the audience members through the whole evolutionary spiral, previewing what it might be like when everything that we know we can do *works*. Images of ourselves becoming a universal humanity flood the screen behind her. We see ourselves in cosmic consciousness. We live in an Earth/Space environment. We are extending our lives, our intelligence, and our capacities.

"Mother Earth," Barbara declares, "is giving birth to a universal humanity. We are entering the new Garden of Co-Creation, where the Tree of Life dwells.

"In the first Garden of Eden, we were embedded in nature and in Spirit. Then we left, for whatever reason we may never know. This we do know: For 50,000 years, we've endured the great Hero's Journey of separation and individuation, until in our age we've penetrated matter itself and discovered the invisible processes of creation—the atom, the gene, the brain.

"We are gaining the power of gods. But if we stay separate from each other, from nature, and from the deeper patterns of creation, we will surely misuse our power and destroy our lives.

"Here, in the Theater for the Future, we step across the threshold, from the land of the separated human into a *new* Garden of Co-Creation. It is the Eighth Day of Creation. On the Seventh Day, God rested and saw that it is good. On the Eighth Day, humanity awoke and realized that we are responsible for our part in the creation."

(*Author's note:* More than 30 years later, this "Eighth Day" scenario would become the "Day One" scenario of the December 2012 event.)

"This is the design of creation. We are meant to learn to be co-creators with the Divine. Our problems—all the challenges facing humanity—are *evolutionary drivers,* waking us up for survival itself, turning us on to our creativity, forcing us to join together (whether we like each other or not), and moving us from the eon of maximum procreation to the next eon of co-creation.

"We are about to discover what it means to be fully human . . . or to self-destruct. In the Garden of Co-Creation, we learn to reconnect with inner Divinity, with nature, with *each other,* and with the whole process of creation. It is the new space in consciousness in which we gain the experience of building a new world equal to our full potential. It is a kindergarten for godlings."

The program ends with a loving depiction of the planetary birth. With Pachelbel's *Canon in D Major* as a musical backdrop and a picture of the "Synergizing Earth" on the screen, lights are shown connecting throughout the planet until the whole world glows. Barbara speaks as the animation concludes . . .

"We are one body. We are universal. We are higher life. We are learning more of God as we understand the processes of creation and become co-creative with them. We are becoming Second Couples at the Tree of Life, uniting whole being with whole being."

The lights come up. In the room, there is a feeling that the earth has become one living body, surrounded by life, and that its people have opened their collective eyes, and smiled together their first planetary smile.

The Program's Effect . . . on Barbara Herself

Whenever Barbara presents this program, with wonderful production assistance from John (who has created the whole technical side of it, actually, based on Barbara's content), something begins to rise up in her.

She describes the experience to her partner.

"It is beyond 'supra-sex,' beyond life purpose. It is Spirit itself. It is the Creator Within. I'm tapping into the Process of Creation and affirming it for our species as a whole."

John smiles and nods his understanding.

"My own biochemical system is taking this seriously!" Barbara exclaims. "As we believe, so it *is* done. John, as I spoke the words in the field of empathy and resonance that we created in that room, my own psychic powers turned on. I was connected through these ideas and the audience with the whole of life. For a moment, I felt that I actually became clairvoyant and telepathic. I believe all the so-called paranormal abilities are inherent in all of us, waiting for the time of deep resonance with the Conscious Force itself to turn us on.

"I felt a taste of 'the hunger of Eve' fulfilled. That hunger is for union with God and all life as part of the process of creation. It is to become co-creators. This is the new feminine archetype being born in us.

"The hunger of Eve had driven me from my life as a Jewish agnostic child through seeker, wife and mother, and futurist toward the discovery of the new story, the new person, the new life, the world . . . a new way of being prefigured by the saints and seers of the human race, and now becoming a new norm in us."

Later, Barbara is to write in her journal:

> Never doubt your own higher guidance. Test it, nurture it, have faith in it. The timing is not in our hands! But here is the secret. The Universe is responsive to requests.
>
> Nothing in our lives is wasted. Not a hair, not a feather, is lost as long as we keep going, following our deepest heart's desire. It is in each one of us to listen, to receive guidance, to act, and to become something more than we ever dreamed we could.
>
> This is the heart of the story we have to tell.

Indeed, it is the heart of the story that Barbara will tell with more vigor than ever for the next three decades. But she could never have even begun to tell it—in this new Theater for the Future or in any other way—had she not made a major shift in her life. The Mystery Story of Barbara's life continues to unravel, showing us that what is happening in every Here-and-Now could not possibly have happened without a There and Then that put all the pieces into place.

⚘ ⚘ ⚘

25.

EPISODE #7: CHANGING IDENTITIES, 1969–1970—
The Years Leading Up to Telling a New Story . . .

What do you do when Who You Are is no longer Who You Were?

I'm aware of only two options in such a situation:

1. Pretend that you are still Who You Were, becoming an actor in a little "play" being produced every day on a tiny stage for an audience of one or two or three, or . . .

2. Be honest, fess up, step into Who You Are now, and deal with the outcome with as much love, patience, courage, and understanding that you can muster.

In the first year of the seventh decade of the 20th century, Barbara Marx Hubbard chose the second option.

The Most Difficult Decision of Her Life

Barbara was simply not happy. And the problem was not that she and Earl Hubbard didn't get along or that she no longer loved her husband. The problem was that Barbara just wasn't satisfied being a housewife and mother. Or I should say, being *only* a housewife and mother. And those seemed to be the only options open to her with Earl.

Earl Hubbard, as it turns out, was a genius—an exciting, daring artist and an insightful, incisive observer of life. His personal brilliance was undeniable. He could talk for hours and never become boring. His life was lived on the edge of his feelings, and his feelings for life itself were always intense, full, and rich with nuance and awareness.

The difficulty was that Barbara, too, was brilliant. And there appeared to only be room in the Hubbard household for one source of brilliance . . . or, at least, for one *public* source.

Earl enjoyed, for sure, Barbara's intellect at home. He loved their morning conversations over breakfast after the children had gone off to school. They sat together for hours talking about the state of the world, the deeper meaning of life, the implications of daily events, the future of humanity, and the co-creative process through which all people everywhere might jointly engage in producing that future. He loved that Barbara always had wonderful, insightful suggestions about whatever he was doing—his canvas art or his public discourses and lectures, for instance.

She had even drawn out of him, by sharp questioning during those breakfast dialogues, what amounted to an entire book including her own extrapolations from Earl's initial take on the ideas they were both exploring. She became his editor, sifting through all of the transcribed ideas, discovering the themes, and turning the words into a book.

Barbara had always had a ton of ideas, a mountain of questions, a pile of observations, and not a small number of genuinely original insights. This had been true since she was a teenager, and it was increasingly so as she moved into her adult life. But . . . she had no place for that voice to be heard.

Earl would listen, of course, and she appreciated that. He paid astute attention; he used her as a sounding board for his own thoughts; and he engaged with her in spontaneous, spirited, and sprightly exchanges that made it clear that he honored and respected her point of view. Indeed, many of her ideas melted—as would be natural under such circumstances—into his own. Similarly, many of his thoughts merged with hers.

The days of her breakfast dialogues with Earl have been described by Barbara as the happiest times of her marriage. Yet as months and years passed, it was not enough for her to watch her ideas fly across the French toast and coffee, be received with enthusiasm, and then go no further . . . except, perhaps, in something she heard Earl himself say in a later talk someplace, in a cocktail-party conversation somewhere, or in an interview with someone.

What Is This Feeling?

It was starting to get to her, the seemingly built-into-the-marriage limitation on her own ability to personally enter the fray where thoughts were being frenetically swapped, where solutions to problems were being proposed, where ideas about a better tomorrow were being conceived. Earl was always in the thick of it in these arenas, with Barbara floating around the edges, acting as, always, the perfect wife, the ideal support person, the busy mother, the wonderful hostess—the one who was seen and not heard.

At first Barbara didn't know what to make of what she was now feeling. Was she simply jealous of her husband? No, of course not. She was far more mature than that. Was it frustration at not having her own ideas honored, or even heard, anywhere outside her home? That was closer to it, but her emotion seemed to have more power than simple frustration.

Was it *anger*? Was she actually becoming *angry* over her voicelessness?

Yes. But even more, it was depression. Something in her wanted to be *expressed,* and she didn't know what. She thought it was only her husband who had ideas, a voice to speak them; and she was doing everything in her power to be sure he was heard.

All of this was in evidence on an evening in October 1970 when it became crystal clear to Barbara that she could no longer choose the option of pretending to be who she once was: the silent wife of a brilliant artist and philosopher; and an editor, promoter, and full-time mom of five wonderful children.

Earl was invited to speak for an entire day to a citizens group in South Carolina, presenting the idea of new worlds. John—being the media relations wizard that he was—had managed to talk the major public-television station there into producing a one-hour documentary based on the talk. As I've done before, I'll let Barbara tell the story from here in her own words, as previously published:

"As Earl was rehearsing and John was busily making arrangements for him, I found my spirits sinking. During the day, a TV crew and Earl went from location to location. Without disturbing Earl, I went to our room and began to cry. I could not handle this raging anger.

"I was shocked to discover that something inside me wanted to speak and would no longer remain silent. That feeling was tearing me apart. When Earl returned after a long day during which he had been well received, he found me red-eyed and exhausted.

"'Barbara, what in the world is wrong?' He tried to embrace me.

"I couldn't bring myself to tell him the truth. 'I don't know, I don't know,' I said. He had worked so hard, and I felt like I was being so unfair. He thought he was pleasing me.

"He took me to dinner alone, and we sat, with him holding my hand, mystified. 'Earl, you did so well, so well,' I blurted out, and then started to weep.

"Finally, he understood. Sighing deeply, he said, 'I know what it is. You want to do it yourself. The more I succeed, the worse you're going to feel.' He was really distressed. You see, I was his only contact with the world. He didn't have a single friend otherwise, male or female."

Barbara initially protested Earl's characterization of her feelings. "That's not true, not true," she remarked. "There's room for us both . . . but I can't be secondary to you anymore." Then it just came out.

"I have to speak for myself."

The Change Proves Too Much

Their relationship could not weather the shift in Barbara. Earl felt displaced and rejected. "I'm doing this all for *you*," he said again. "I'm the genius, you are the editor!"

But they both realized that no one else can make another person happy. Barbara had to do it for herself.

The shift eventually led to separation and an end to their marriage. The divorce was painful for Earl and the couple's children. In notes to me for this book, Barbara said, "I regret that I didn't have the skill or the way to continue living by expanding my role as wife, mother, editor, and helper. Now, 30 years later, I can see that it's somewhat easier for young couples. Many men realize that women are equals. And the best men welcome the emerging power of women. They know the planet needs us. They know that men alone cannot solve the problems of the world, but need the balance and activation of feminine energy.

"And now, because of the success of the women's movement, especially in the developed world, women are not motivated so much by anger or the desire for equality as they are moved by the yearning to give of their creativity for the good of the world.

"This is the new archetype of the feminine co-creator. Her longing is for co-equal co-creation with her beloved, for partnership. Her desire is for deeper union, whole being with whole being. She is making the fateful shift from self-reproduction to self-evolution, life purpose, chosen work, and chosen children.

"Her role is expanding from procreation to co-creation. This means being motivated from within by the creative impulse to give one's unique gift to others for the good of the self and the world.

"Without realizing it, I was part of the rising tide of feminine co-creativity drawn forth just at the time of the 'planetary birth' when that energy is essential for the survival of the species. I can see now that as we have fewer children and live longer lives, feminine energy is being liberated.

"It is the age of the woman. And it is also the age of the birth of the co-creative man. The liberation of the feminine co-creator paves the way for the freeing of men from the overwhelming burdens of the patriarchy. No longer called to be the predator, the protector, the sole earner, men are liberating themselves to tap into their own deeper creativity and give their unique gifts to the world in ever more unique ways—thereby rendering those gifts far more powerful in the producing of outcomes than the simple instrument of brute force.

"It is co-creative *couples* that are becoming the basis of today's emerging evolutionary society."

I believe that Barbara's assessment is correct. We see it everywhere we look in today's society. But in the earliest days of her own emergence, it wasn't that way. She was one of the early liberators of that feminine energy and remains to this day one of the templates for its full expression.

I believe, further, that her own life and the events in it were specially designed to create the possibility of her *being* one of the templates.

For instance, would Barbara Marx Hubbard's marriage have failed if the history-making flight of American astronaut John Glenn had not succeeded? Would Barbara's friendship with an Air Force colonel who came into her life out of nowhere have blossomed if the first orbit of *Friendship 7* had decayed?

Those are very good questions.

26.

Barbara had been touched in a very deep way on a day in February 1962 when John Glenn blasted into space aboard *Friendship 7*. Glenn was the first American to orbit Earth. She made an entry in her journal about it: "It is a rare experience to watch a species at the precise moment of change, of evolution . . . most of which has been buried in the imperceptible crawl of time past."

Barbara was appalled that virtually no one else shared her view. She wrote: "Many intellectuals don't consider the adventure into space important. They say it will never change humanity's condition, yet it's as true as saying that the discovery of fire made no difference—of course it will change our condition. It will change humanity itself to have achieved this. How else are we changed than by what we do and where we do it?"

She held these ideas within her, where they grew like seeds in a garden in the very early spring, and said little to anyone for four years. But in 1966, Barbara had an epiphany that solidified her view of the space program and its place in humanity's evolution. It was a mystical hilltop experience—her life's first major spiritual encounter—in which she had a vision that affected the remainder of her life.

To her, it now seemed clear that humanity's burst into outer space was a significant part of a much larger process, an in-the-moment outpicturing of an evolutionary impulse. Barbara saw all that was happening around the world as part of a normal evolutionary process that she experienced as our *birth* as a living planetary species just becoming aware of itself as a whole, while being born into a universe of trillions of planetary systems, some of which may have life comparable to our own.

She found herself talking about this one day with her friend Natalie—Lady Malcolm Douglas-Hamilton, a widow who had organized Bundles for Britain during World War II and was now setting up the Center of American Living, an effort to affirm cultural excellence in the United States. Barbara told Natalie that she felt a deep urge to wake people up to the immense significance of humanity's ventures off the earth, and the remarkable potential of the space program to catapult the human race to a new level in its own evolution.

She didn't have much of a platform in her own life as a housewife and mother to actually get something done, she knew, but she couldn't help but wish. . . .

"Why don't we have a space meeting?" Natalie suggested brightly.

"A what?" Barbara asked.

"A space meeting. We could invite civic leaders, and leaders in the space program, to sit down together at a conference right here in New York and see if we can't get them to view the larger picture, and then to work together."

"Yes!" Barbara exclaimed. "They could cooperate in creating a *citizen-based global cooperative space program* to shift the genius of the military-industrial complex from war to new worlds on Earth and new worlds in space."

Barbara was thrilled!

She proceeded to send invitations to everybody and anybody she'd ever heard of in the space program. Natalie, meanwhile, was inviting civic leaders from across the country.

"Coincidence" Plays Its Role . . . Again

The invitations from Barbara and Natalie were circulating widely; and Lt. Col. John Whiteside, chief officer of information for the Air Force in New York City, was asked to look into what the two women were planning and "see if there is anything in it for the Air Force."

He gave the assignment to his assistant, Air Force Captain William Knowlton—and it might have ended there, had "fate" not intervened again. This seemed, after all, to be just two ladies from New York society who wanted to get important people together to sit down and talk—about *what,* they didn't even know. . . .

But when Col. Whiteside slid the invitation letter across the desk and asked Capt. Knowlton to check up on it, his assistant stopped short.

"Wait a minute, I've met this woman. She lives *just down the street from me,*" he told his boss. "I don't know her well, but I've met her, and she's not someone who's 'way out there.' You might want to talk with her."

"Okay, so go see what you can find out."

Knowlton did, ringing the Hubbard's doorbell in suburban Lakeville, Connecticut, that weekend, asking if he might come in for a visit to talk about what Mrs. Hubbard was planning. Barbara invited him in, and Earl joined them in the living room. They talked for over an hour about the meaning of space and the future of humankind.

Their own previous breakfast dialogues made it clear to both Barbara and Earl that each deeply believed that exploring "new worlds" was an inevitable aspect of humanity's evolutionary journey, and so Earl was very comfortable as part of the discussion. The Air Force captain was very comfortable, too, appearing to be genuinely impressed. Returning to his office Monday morning, he told Col. Whiteside: "You definitely want to meet with these people." His boss agreed to do so.

Loony Lady or Wondrous Woman?

At the time, Barbara was keeping a small apartment in New York City, and when Col. Whiteside telephoned, she and Earl invited the officer to meet them there for lunch.

Now there he sits, all pressed and creased and *official* in a snappy uniform bottomed by shoes in which you can see your reflection, listening to a couple of private citizens—not connected with NASA or the government in any way—tell him how important the space program is.

Actually, Earl is doing most of the talking, but Barbara does manage to get in a word here and there—and one thing she says nearly stops the show.

"It's like a birth—that is what it's really like," she enthuses. "Humanity is going to be universal."

Col. Whiteside, sitting next to her on the apartment couch, shoots her a glance, blinks once, and then squints in a way that Barbara will one day become very familiar with. Just now, though, she shrinks a bit. Had she jumped to the birth analogy too fast? Does this military officer think that he's just met the Loony Lady of Lakeville?

"It is a natural evolutionary step in the emergence of a universal species," she explains more calmly.

"That is *exactly right*," the Air Force officer erupts, and his expression telegraphs his obvious delight at finding someone else who sees it the way he does. "That's why I was so adamant that all the launches be covered live." He goes on: "They didn't want to do it. The NASA suits didn't want to do it, the military brass didn't want to do it, and the network newsboys didn't want to do it."

Barbara's mind stops its worrying. She tries to grab on to what he dangled out there. "But they *are* being reported live, aren't they?"

"They are *now*. But at the beginning, the space program was being covered as if it were a story about *technology*—lots of still pictures, talking heads, and bunches of facts and data. It was like reporting the birth of Christ by focusing on how much he weighed and how many animals were in the manger. I knew this story was more significant, *much* more significant, than that. I kept urging the networks and the Air Force to have every launch covered live."

John explains that the military brass and NASA officials weren't happy with the idea because if something went wrong, they certainly didn't want instant live coverage of it. And the networks weren't giggly because of the huge cost of location coverage. Eventually, however, he managed to convince both sides to commit to live reporting, arguing that humanity's space launches were not merely wonderful technological achievements, but events of enormous social, historical, and evolutionary importance.

It is not lost on the colonel as he is talking that this is exactly the point that these two noninvolved citizens were making—with Barbara's birth analogy carrying particular impact.

"You don't know one end of a rocket from another," Col. Whiteside smiles. "How did you come to this?"

"I discovered it through my search for meaning," Barbara replies softly.

Impressing the Not-So-Easily Impressed

"You have been searching for the meaning of the space program?"

"No. I've been searching for the meaning of all this *power* we have, all this *technology* we have, and all this *ability* the human race has that is *represented* in the space program."

She gives him a fast-as-she-can sketch of what she calls the New Story—not mentioning to him, of course, that it all came to her as part of a spiritual encounter.

She ends with an assessment of the space program as the first truly significant and highly visible act in humanity's evolution.

Barbara's perception of the liftoff of rockets as the launching of a new universal species and Earl's almost lecture-like dissertation on why finding New Worlds is humanity's next evolutionary step has captivated the Air Force officer.

"And now I know that it's not enough to talk about it," Barbara asserts. "People like us, outside the space program—citizens—have to *act*. There are advocates for every disease, every need, but not for the *future of humanity*."

She's catching his attention again. The way she *reasons*, the way she phrases things, is making a deep impression. And this is a man of the world, someone who has been around and who isn't easily impressed. John looks at Barbara almost analytically now. *What does this lady really want?* he wonders. *What's her bottom line?*

"We've got to learn how to communicate meaning for the future," she concludes, as if reading his mind. Col. Whiteside shakes his head sadly. "I'm an Air Force officer for information, and do you know what I'm trying to communicate about now? The C-5!" He laughs derisively. "The F-111. And the *Vietnam War*." His laughter melts as the lines on his face deepen.

There's a beat. The colonel's eyes meet Barbara's. He squints at her in a way that seems strangely personal. *Uh-oh*, Barbara says to herself. *What's this?*

(Years later, she would admit to feeling a surprising attraction for him at that first lunch. "He was masculine and sexy," she wrote. "There were no other words for it. He was a man who knew women easily. His look of self-confidence, intelligence, exuberance, and natural leadership charmed me.")

The Effects of All This

John's entrance into Barbara's life played a catalytic effect on her dramatic change of identity from her husband's editor, Connecticut housewife, and mother of five to nationally recognized futurist and spokesperson for the potential of tomorrow.

In John Whiteside, Barbara had met another very powerful and brilliant man—but one with a singular and important difference from her powerful and brilliant husband. John Whiteside would demonstrate the ability to share life's stage, to make room for co-creation, to experience a *partnership* of brilliance. He didn't seek to be the only one in the spotlight.

Maybe it was the fact that he had already spent years center stage as someone "out front" in the world's biggest media market, whereas Earl Hubbard was still trying to find his land legs after wallowing in a sea of indifference about his ideas and art from the media and public at large. Fair enough. Whatever the reasons, John's encouragement and nurturing of Barbara as a new friend stood in contrast to the only role she could play in her marriage with which Earl seemed comfortable: wife, mother, and steadfast supporter of his work—and his work alone.

Barbara, meanwhile, was grappling with a vision on a hilltop in 1966 that brought her two things: a new story about humanity as compelling as any story our species has ever told itself *about* itself; *and* . . . an invitation, indeed, what she felt was an *imperative*, to *tell* the story to the world. This, in order to awaken the world to its own process, thus aiding the process itself and ensuring our species would know that its crisis is a birth. It is one planetary system able to coordinate itself as a whole, waking up to its entry into the universe, possibly into a cosmic community of Universal Beings, even though she had no experience of this possibility.

Earl simply didn't understand any of this. He didn't fully comprehend the level of urgency within his wife to find her voice and use it beyond the breakfast-table dialogues that the two enjoyed so much. He could not for the life of him figure out why the woman he married and had five children with could not be content to just stay at home and be a good wife and attentive mother . . . as well as his inspiration, editor, promoter, and muse.

This was the 1950s model of "wifedom" and marriage; and to Earl, it all seemed perfectly reasonable. And because Barbara loved and respected her husband immensely, she bought into the model. He *was* a genius (she wasn't making that up just because she married him), and he *did* need support to be successful. His paintings were stark art, portraits of people as faces glowing with the white light of awareness in a background of universal black. He had done just such a painting of Barbara, and it was not gratuitous. He did see her as a woman very aware and insightful. Their talks every morning proved this. Yet he wanted her to be the

"Behind every great man, there is a great woman" kind of wife; and now—suddenly, abruptly, surprisingly—that wasn't enough for her.

A Breath of Fresh Air

Barbara did try—she really did for nearly 18 years—to fit into the cultural pattern of the 1950s: PTA, League of Women Voters, French cooking, housecleaning, taking the children on walks, reading and singing to them, and all the wonderful things that mothers do . . . 24 hours a day, 7 days a week. But by the mid-'60s, she realized that she was dying inside. She knew it before then, actually, but this is when she first began to admit it to herself. She had too much to offer, too much to say, too much that she felt *needed* to be said. And now here was John Whiteside, a man apparently holding the strange notion that Barbara Marx Hubbard was *supposed* to be saying it, not simply sitting around smiling.

The first sign of this came shortly after the initial visit between Earl, Barbara, and John over lunch. Capt. Knowlton called to say that Col. Whiteside wondered if he could have a dozen copies of the book *The Search Is On,* which Barbara had edited for Earl from their breakfast dialogues. With this show of continuing interest in her and Earl's thoughts, Barbara called the colonel and asked him to help her with the "space meeting."

Unlike Earl, who was scornful and critical of the idea of Barbara trying to act upon their ideas personally—rather than simply communicating them through him—John's immediate reaction was: "Let's do it, Barbara!" The contrast in energy was immediately refreshing.

"I knew I had found the person I needed," she was to write later. "We began to work together. He took over the organization of the meeting, the invitations, and the media contacts."

Barbara didn't leave it at that. She wanted the colonel's help with a much larger agenda: her life mission to tell the story of humanity's birth—and to tell it *in the first person,* not through someone else. She saw John's organizational skills and production abilities and asked if he would join her in her vocation.

Barbara knew that John already agreed with her vision, with her characterization, of both the space program and *all* that was happening in the world contemporarily as part of the process of humanity's evolution. She also knew from his comments that his present work of trying to "sell" the media on weapons of war and the Vietnam conflict were not fulfilling his soul.

And so she wondered whether John would join her in creating and delivering this new understanding of humanity's larger purpose and possible future. An understanding that called to the best in people and spoke to, and *from,* their soul—a story that was meant to happen, not just to be talked about. . . .

John at first pulled back from the idea. It would require him to retire again from the Air Force (he had already done so once, to form his own successful advertising firm, but he was called back when the Korean War broke out). But his first reluctance had more to do with what he felt were his own personal characteristics. He didn't think he had the high standards of morality necessary to work on a project as spiritually sourced as Barbara's birth-of-humanity vision. He was a Southern Baptist, and he told her that he was a "sinner."

On this score, Barbara had no illusions. She could see that John was a hard-living, hard-drinking, hard-partying man. (The fact that he was married didn't seem to stop him.) Yet it was precisely because he was such a "man of the world" that she felt he might be more effective in placing *into* the world a new story *about* the world. There was nothing self-righteous or "perfect" about John Whiteside. And in some ways, that made him, ironically, the "perfect" person to help in getting out the message of how this imperfect world could turn itself around, at last, and use its power to create a more ideal planet. She tried to convince him of that.

John thought it over for several weeks. Then he called his new friend the moment he'd made up his mind, saying, "Barbara, I've decided to do it. I'm going to give my life full-time to this." He made the call exactly when he'd made the decision, probably to avoid rethinking it and going back on it. That's how the call happened to be on the evening of December 24, 1969.

And so, in some soft symmetry, it was on Christmas Eve that he followed the impulse to drop everything and fully enter her life . . . and it was on Christmas Eve a dozen years later that he dropped everything and fully left.

REFLECTIONS & EXPLORATIONS

The Two Most Important Questions in a Relationship

As we reflect on the times just described, and look more close-ly at Barbara's experience to see what we all might benefit from, we are reminded that . . .

> . . . **there are only two questions to ask in every relationship:** *Where am I going?* **and** *Who is going with me?* **It is important to** *never reverse the order of the questions.*

This is the most vital, "on the nose" information I've ever re-ceived about creating lifelong partnerships.

Many of us experience romantic encounters that we fantasize turning into long-term companionships and even marriages, yet we fail to ask these two questions. Or, worse yet, we ask them in the wrong order.

If we ask them in reverse order, we often wind up asking what *should* have been the *first* question over and over again for the next several years—until we realize that we simply are not happy. We are not okay (perhaps *very* not okay) with the direction in which

205

our life is moving—even though we still very much love the person we are with.

Somehow we got sidetracked. And somewhere two or three years down the road, we look into the mirror and wonder what happened to our Selves. Where did all those dreams that we had for ourselves go?

The difficulty with this is that after a while—once you become clear that you aren't living the life you wanted—you may become surly, irritable, and moody. Your partner, of course, will wonder what's going on and will ask. And you can't say that anything in particular is "wrong"—you just know that nothing feels "quite right."

Soon, this feeling permeates your relationship, and with luck, that relationship changes in its form, or is over in its present form. (No relationship ever truly ends; it simply changes form as time passes. That includes relationships in which people continue living together. If you are lucky, you can shift the form of your relationship, either on your own or with the help of a good counselor.)

If you're not lucky, the relationship will continue in its present unhappy, unsatisfying, and unfulfilling form for a long time— and you'll live a life of quiet desperation. More marriages than you might guess fall into this category.

How can that cycle be broken? By asking yourself those two questions, no *matter at what point in the relationship you find yourself.* In other words, they are not questions to ask only at the outset, only when you are considering entering into a new partnership. These can be asked at *any time.* So here are those questions again:

1. *Where am I going?*

2. *Who is going with me?*

Now the fact is that most people *do* ask themselves these questions at one time or another, but many make the mistake of putting the questions *in reverse order.* That's why I'm making such a point of it here. They ask the second question first; or they may have them in good order when they first meet someone, but then they change the order of the questions around so that they can get a better answer!

If you do either of these things, you may encounter great difficulty in relationships.

What Barbara's life teaches us is that the life agenda of those to whom we find ourselves attracted is critically important in the choice of life mates. Now that may seem like an almost ridiculously obvious and simplistic observation, but obvious or simplistic as it may be, it is a factor that only a tiny percentage of people "in love" pay any attention to—until it is way too late.

It is true, as well, that people change. Their dreams change, their desires change, their understandings about life change, their levels of awareness change, their purpose, and their very reason for living can even change (as in the case of Barbara). Which brings us to a second great teaching about life: It is very important for all of us to understand that . . .

. . . there is no such thing as a permanent answer to anything.

If you think that the answer you got today is the answer you are always going to get tomorrow, then you don't know how life works. *Everything changes.* Change is the nature of Life itself. Even your *own* answers—the answers you give *yourself* to the questions you *ask* yourself—change over time. So you must be prepared for change, and prepared to embrace it gracefully. It is a life skill that Barbara developed as her own life moved forward. As her story here shows, she has for the past 50 years always been light on her feet.

You have to be light on your feet if you're going to dance with angels. . . .

We will explore this truth deeply on the pages ahead, through the telling of more and more of Barbara's story.

Enjoy.

🌿 🌿 🌿

Barely six months after they'd met, John Whiteside had become what Barbara called "a great new factor in my life." She and Earl began to travel the country with him, presenting the "new worlds" idea to local Lions Clubs, Kiwanis Clubs, Exchange Clubs—any group that would give them an audience.

Earl became the spokesperson. Barbara edited speeches for him out of their morning dialogues, and John handled all the advance work and on-the-road arrangements, as well as media contacts and press conferences. But the approach wasn't working well. Earl's tendency to address the topic as an absolutist wasn't very effective on the hustings—especially with generals or the news media. (His whole energy projected that *of course* this was humanity's answer for a sane future . . . *of course* we had to spend the money and use the resources to find other inhabitable bodies in space. How could there be any question about it, much less any disagreement?)

It wasn't long before John began speaking to Barbara privately about it. "We can't keep putting Earl out there as the spokesperson," he would say. "He's killing the energy. He's hurting feelings and making people feel small if they raise the slightest question or objection regarding any part of what he is saying. He's prickly and cold with audiences, and this isn't going to work."

"Well, John, he *is* eloquent on the subject. Who else can speak with such articulation on all this?"

"*You* can, Barbara. You can, and you know it. And what's more, you can do it with warmth, lighthearted humor, and a sense of compassion about where people are. Your genuine excitement is infectious. I'm sorry, but Earl is not *infectious*—he is *infecting*. He's an amazing thinker and a brilliant man, but his place is not in front of an audience."

The road trip continued as it was, however, until the trio returned home in late spring. Then Barbara and John had an idea to create The Committee for the Future. They invited friends and acquaintances, including some of the heads of the media to whom John had earlier introduced Barbara. A distinguished group from various fields met at the Hubbard house in Lakeville for the Committee's founding meeting in June 1970. It was just eight months after their first luncheon meeting the previous October.

A Marriage Ends—a New Partnership Begins

Barbara was experiencing something with John that she hadn't experienced before: co-creation. She began falling in love with John. She also loved her husband, and she struggled inside. Could she love both men, each in a different way, without compromising her marriage?

She and John went on to create other projects together. Given his vast experience with the media, his inherent problem-solving ability, and his highly polished communication skills (if you can communicate philosophical ideas effectively inside the *military establishment,* you can communicate effectively *anywhere*), his gifts combined wonderfully with Barbara's in finding a striking way to *physicalize* what had been largely a conceptualization.

They worked on something called Harvest Moon (an idea to get regular citizens involved in space, which would have the effect of generating huge support for a program that continued to be criticized in many quarters as a pointless boondoggle), as well as the SYNCONS. Those "synergistic convergence" meetings—the forerunner of the Day One event—were perhaps the biggest contribution John made to Barbara's outside-the-house life.

The conceptual basis of the "SYNCON" was not John's idea. For years, Barbara had been talking about the need to create synergistic energy to solve the world's many problems and meet its challenges. Indeed, the whole push to get average citizens directly involved in the space program was a manifestation of that awareness. But, typical of the role John always played, he was able to take this broad idea of creating *synergy* and help Barbara give it shape and substance.

This "shaping" began as the two met with industrialists, politicians, ambassadors, and others from many walks of life to promote a new national goal: "New Worlds on Earth, New Worlds in Space: A 30-Year Global Cooperative Earth/Space Human Development Process."

So often they heard from members of one group or the other: "I get this, I believe this, but you'll never get a politician (or business leader, student, or member of one of the other groups) to get it." In other words, people had stereotyped opinions of each other that were often simply wrong.

One day John drew a circle on a napkin. "How about building a wheel and inviting everyone who disagrees with everyone else to meet in the wheel?" he suggested. "Let's have sectors of basic functions like health, education, economics, and the environment. Let's invite leaders at the growing edge of the sciences and psychologies. Let's have artists help us see that we are becoming . . ." and he drew the first SYNCON Wheel.

Using this model, SYNCON meetings were held across the country—which John booked, organized, and produced, putting Barbara in front of the room while he stood in the back.

Barbara suddenly felt seen, heard, and energized. She hired a full-time nanny for her children and began holding more meetings, traveling to more and more places, and even giving interviews. She was, indeed, finding her own voice for the first time since her marriage in 1951.

With all the traveling and her emergence as a kind of "spokesperson for tomorrow," Barbara and Earl began to grow apart. After some months they were, *ipso facto,* separated. For reasons private to his own experience, John had already withdrawn from his marriage as well. Soon, Barbara and John became a couple. A *co-creative* couple. His talents and hers seemed to fuse perfectly. He continued to be just great at putting on the ground what Barbara carried around in her head. And his constant phrase whenever she had an idea was: "Let's do it!"—words Barbara had been waiting to hear.

The two asked Barbara's sister Jacqueline if they might live for a while in her beautiful mansion called Greystone, which was in Rock Creek Park near Washington, D.C. She had been lending it to family members. Hidden in the park, it had white pillars, a grape arbor, and a tennis court. Jacqueline agreed; and Barbara, her children, and John moved to Washington.

"Greystone became a center for conscious evolution," Barbara shared with me for this book. "It was an oasis of the future in the midst of the nation's capital. We invited colleagues to visit us, and they came from all over the world to tell their stories of what is emerging, what is new, what is possible."

About Those SYNCONS . . .

In those discussions with Barbara for this book, I asked her to give me one more pass at those SYNCONS that she and John had worked so hard on. I wanted to make sure that I really "got" the whole idea, since it seemed to have come to its fullest development and grandest application—finally—as the Wheel of Co-Creation in the Synergy Engine created for unveiling as part of the Day One event on December 22, 2012.

"Well, it was actually a new kind of *conferencing process* that we invented," Barbara explained. "We called it, almost jokingly, a 'SYNCON' for Synergistic Convergence. The Air Force had a penchant for coming up with abbreviated code names for everything it did, and John simply couldn't help himself. The name stuck, and we brought all kinds of people together in wheels constructed by students in universities to look at goals, needs, and resources in the light of the growing potential of the whole system.

"The SYNCON Wheel represents the whole human community self-organized into *a new emerging system* based on people's desire to co-create and synergize to achieve their own goals. Ambassadors, Nobel Prize–winning scientists, hippies, welfare mothers, environmentalists, and developers—everybody who disagreed with everybody—received an invitation into the SYNCON Wheel.

"When each functional group (such as Health, Education, Economics, Environment, Science and Technology, Arts, and Media) shared its goals, needs, and resources with the others, we took down all the walls that had been placed between sectors. Individuals were asked to look for common goals and match needs with resources."

Barbara said that every time they did this, people felt the energy of cooperation and connection build. This feeling, she explained, emerges whenever there is "synergy"—the coming together of separate parts to build a new, greater whole.

"This is the way nature works. Everything interacts synergistically. This is the way nature takes leaps. And what we were doing was adapting this evolutionary form to *social interactions,* creating a way for separate groups and individuals to better achieve their own goals through cooperation rather than opposition."

Each SYNCON event—and Barbara and John held them around the country—featured that All Walls Down Ceremony, when the walls between sectors of the Wheel were taken down in preparation for the group assembling as a whole. Barbara remarked, smiling, "It was phenomenal. It was like a social love affair. People danced and sang. We reassembled in the Wheel as members of the whole, with the leading-edge scientists and psychologists telling us about new potentials, while each group discussed a better way to achieve its goals through greater cooperation.

"We were discovering the process of a more synergistic democracy. SYNCONS were designed to assist each individual in realizing his or her goals through connecting with others who needed what that person had to give."

Barbara even had a new word for this: *Synocracy,* or synergistic, cooperative democracy. "We were laying down a template that might contribute toward the next step in self-governance, I believe."

The Effect They Had

I asked Barbara if she could give me an example of how SYNCON broke down walls, not just in the wheels that had been created for each event, but in people's hearts and minds.

"Oh, I could give you many of them," she said. "At one SYNCON, during the Assembly of the Whole, when this social love affair was taking place—with everyone seated in his or her sector of the Wheel now realizing the connections with one another—silence suddenly fell upon the group. A young man, who had been trying unsuccessfully to persuade everyone that marijuana should be legalized for recreational use, had entered the center of the Wheel in his ragged blue jeans and knelt down. He just looked up at all of us, breathed deeply, and said, 'This is what I meant. This is what I really meant all the time. . . .'

"He gave up his plea for marijuana and joined the team of young people building wheels for the next SYNCON.

"At another SYNCON, Edgar Mitchell, the astronaut and founder of the Institute of Noetic Sciences, said that if we had had a spiritual Geiger counter, it would have gone off the charts. The root of the word *religion* is *religare,* meaning 'to restrain or tie back.' SYNCONS brought all of us together in one whole greater than the sum of our parts. The binding energy is the same that brought atom to atom and molecule to molecule."

Barbara said that many times at the SYNCONS, she had the realization that if God is love, then God must be the magnetic power that connects us. She said that as people engaged in the process, they became excited because more of their *potential was released* through joining than through fighting. "They could see the possibility of creating peace through co-creation, peace through the release of human creativity for self-expression, joined."

My God, Barbara thought, *if this process ever took hold and expanded, it would be the alternative to war!*

A New Kind of Life-Giving Energy?

It was during the period when she and John were producing SYNCONS that Barbara discovered what she came to call "supra-sex." She talked about that, too, you may remember, in our first interview in my kitchen in Ashland, describing it as "a great new drive in nature."

Looking later at notes that Barbara shared with me from her journals, I found this:

> Just as we reproduced the species by joining together to create, now we will evolve the species by joining to co-create.
>
> And since we are overpopulated and must have fewer children, the drive to self-reproduce is expanding into the desire to self-evolve . . . especially in women, for the sake of the survival of our children.
>
> My hormones were turning on again—this time to give birth to my own creativity through joining with others. The great drives for self-preservation and self-reproduction are expanding into the third great drive: *self-evolution and the fulfillment of our greater potential.*
>
> This is the way toward the Hunger of Eve fulfilled.

The Family Doesn't Get It

The supra-sexual drive really took hold of Barbara. She was aflame with the desire to express and create. She fell in love with the potential of herself and of all people to come together and realize their full potential. "In doing the SYNCONS, I became a Feminine Co-Creator. I experienced a taste of the new world," is how she put it.

Her family was not nearly as enthusiastic. In fact, they thought she was crazy, spending money going around the world building "wheels" everywhere she could. Barbara didn't care. Now ultra-energized, she founded the New Worlds Training and Education Center and initiated an evolutionary educational program. About ten young people moved into Greystone, where Barbara and John had the school, a conference center, and a team working to produce SYNCONS throughout the world, from the island nation of Jamaica to the inner city of Los Angeles with gang leaders.

By the end of the 1970s, Barbara had completely changed her identity. She was being seen and hailed as a "futurist."

"People think that futurists wear silver suits and have antennae coming out of their heads," she quipped, chuckling with interviewers who started calling her. "But a futurist is simply an expanded parent. When a couple becomes pregnant, they look ahead at least 20 years. Now we are all parents of our own future on planet Earth."

Everything that had occurred during that tumultuous, shift-producing decade from 1969 to 1979 emerged from something that happened to Barbara on a hilltop in Connecticut.

Nothing pops out of nowhere. Everything proceeds from what precedes.

28.

EPISODE #6: THE BIRTH REVELATION, 1966—
Three Years Prior to Changing Identities . . .

It was Barbara's habit to take a little walk every day after lunch, cold or warm, rain or shine (well, if it was *pouring,* she certainly didn't go, but if it was just a light drizzle . . .). It was a break in her routine with five children and increasing outside activities and commitments. It was a time to clear her head and rest her mind and, well, just not have to *do anything.* For a few blessed minutes each day, she allowed herself some *sanity time,* where the world didn't ask for anything except to be seen . . . where life didn't demand a thing, but merely invited the softest kind of participation —the pointless participation of objectiveless observation. Just being and seeing, with no need to *do* anything except to be and to see.

One afternoon in February 1966, she was taking just such a walk, moving slowly and gently, up a small hill near her Lakeville, Connecticut, home. Now, just as I did with The Christ Experience, I'm going to let Barbara take it from here, sharing this moment with us in her own words, which were previously published.

From Barbara's Own Written Description . . .

It was a freezing day. The trees stood black and brittle against the winter sky. There was no sign of life anywhere. I wrapped my scarf around my face to protect myself from the bitter cold and walked with my head down to avoid the wind.

I had been reading Reinhold Neibuhr on the subject of community. He had quoted St. Paul's famous statement: "All men are members of one body." I was thinking about that idea and feeling a deep nameless frustration in my own body, as if an awareness were poised, flickering just beyond the periphery of my consciousness, attempting to enter my mind. I felt envious of the Gospel writers. They had a simple story to tell: A child was born and all the rest followed from that. Peasants and kings could understand it. Western civilization was built on it. *One story!*

Searching for a Metaphor; Seeking Out the Story

Unexpectedly, a question burst forth from the depth of my being. I spoke it out loud, almost in anger as though I could not live without knowing the answer. Lifting my voice to the ice-white sky, I demanded to know: "What is *our* story? What in our age is comparable to the birth of Christ?"

I lapsed into a daydreamlike state, walking without thinking around the top of the hill. Suddenly, my mind's eye penetrated the blue cocoon of Earth and lifted me up into the utter blackness of outer space. A Technicolor movie turned on.

I felt the earth as a living organism, heaving for breath, struggling to coordinate itself as one body. *It was alive!* I became a cell in the body. The pain of the whole body was flashing through the mass media, the nervous system of the world.

I felt the children starving, soldiers dying, mothers crying, people burning. The agony of our earth was mine. Her polluted waters, her clogged air, her depleted soil, her decimated forests . . . it was all happening to *me!* She and I were one. There was no other, no outside. We were one body.

Then the movie sped up, and I saw something new. A flash of extraordinary light, more radiant than the sun, gleamed in outer space. Instantly, all of us, collectively, were attracted to the light. We forgot our pain for the moment. We stopped crying, and together we saw the light. It caught our attention for one brief instant.

With that *moment of shared attention,* empathy began to course through our bodies. Wave upon wave of love flowed through all people. A magnetic *field* of love aligned us. We were caressed, uplifted in this field of light. Joy began to pulse around and through us.

We felt light rising from within. Miracles and healings occurred. The blind could see, the lame could walk, the deaf could hear. People flooded out of their homes, offices, and buildings, meeting each other in ever-growing gatherings . . . embracing, singing, and loving one another. We sang together in spontaneous harmonies, a planetary choir of voices singing out loud for the first time. A chanting rhythm beat through the earth, synchronizing our heartbeats.

No division of race, color, nation, or class held against the pressure of attraction. The ancient human feelings of separation and fear dissolved as waves of love pulled us to each other. Our hearts opened, our thoughts connected, and we experienced *the awesome intelligence of ourselves as one living body.*

I saw the weapons melt. The air cleared, the waters purified, the land renewed. I could breathe again. Food coursed through the body, reaching *all* our members. The pain of the earth dissolved. The *mass media pulsed with light.* As it carried the stories of our transformation, *it was transformed.*

I saw our rockets rising majestically, penetrating the blue sky, *silver slivers of life,* reaching beyond our terrestrial home to the place where my mind's eye resided. In the universal dark, they were *carrying the seed of humanity* in peace to our cosmic destiny as children of the stars.

As the rockets penetrated outer space, the earth coordinated itself as one body. Reaching outward and aligning our bodies were *one gesture.* Just as a baby's reach for an object outside its own body helps it coordinate, so our reach into space was speeding up the integration of all of our systems on the planet. I felt it in my own body.

With each wave of harmony, the glowing light surrounding us intensified. As we grew together as One, the light became brighter and seemed to fuse with the light within each of us. We were growing brighter as we joined. As we connected on Earth, millions of distant points of lifelike light became visible in the Universe, surrounding us. As we harmonized, they became more visible. As we became One, they became Real.

We heard a *tone*—a vibration that oriented us in one direction. The entire human race was magnetized by that sound. We were listening together to hear our First Word. The glowing light around our planet seemed to be intelligent, loving, familiar. It was about to speak to us directly. We were straining to understand, yet too immature to fully know the meaning of the sound.

Then I heard these words clearly:

> *Our story is a birth. It is the birth of humankind as One Body. What Christ and all other avatars came to Earth to reveal is true. We are One Body, born into the Universe.*

Then I heard . . .

> *Barbara, go tell the story of our birth!*

The Story Unfolds

With those words, billions of us opened our collective eyes and smiled a *planetary smile!* It was like the first smile of a newborn baby when her little nervous system finally links up. She opens her eyes; sees her mother; and produces that amazing, radiant smile.

Somehow she knows her mother, even though she has never before seen her face-to-face. As that infant knows her mother, so humankind knows the light. Even though we have never seen it together, each of us in a secret place in our hearts has experienced the light. Now, for the first time, we are seeing it as One, through our collective vision. Ecstatic joy rippled throughout the planetary body.

I was enthralled. I shouted to myself upon the hill: "We are being born! It's true! Our *story* . . . is a *birth*. I know it because it's happening to me right now."

A sense of overwhelming gratitude filled me. Then the whole story of our birth unfolded within me, and I felt myself tumbling through an evolutionary spiral. With each advance, I experienced a new turn on the spiral. The creation of the Universe, the earth, single-cell life, multicellular life, human life . . . and now us, going around the spiral once again. It all raced before my inner eye.

First I heard music, then silence more profound than quietness. Then came the awesome thunder of creation. The same tone that had coursed through the planet aligning us at our birth sounded the note at the beginning of time/space.

I felt the coming together of clouds of hydrogen, bursting into supernova, giant stars fusing within their heart of heat . . . the materials of our planet, the minerals and metals that now make up our bodies. I was a large molecule floating passively in the sea of the early earth, suddenly swept up into a new, more complex pattern of life—a cell.

I could see! I could move! I could act! I could even replicate myself!

We continued dividing to reproduce, semi-immortal creatures who did not die. We consumed the nutrients of the terrestrial seas. We began to pollute, overpopulate, and stagnate. We were reaching a limit to growth, coming to the end of the dominance of single-cell life.

Then I felt us coming together as multicellular organisms, joining with one another to face the crisis. We were fusing into new bodies, transforming from single cells to plants, insects, fish, animals, and birds. We invented photosynthesis and built the biosphere; we colonized the once barren earth; we filled every nook and cranny with life. And we learned to die so that our offspring could live on.

Then the first humans appeared. We felt strange in the animal world. We recognized our own death and sought to overcome it.

We heard the voices of gods, we buried food with our dead, we reached for the stars. Then we humans began to replicate even more rapidly. We spanned the earth, learned to mimic nature, and built technological extensions of ourselves until we started to deplete the resources of our Mother Earth.

Our current crisis appeared. Limits to growth! Don't be fruitful and multiply! Cooperate or die! We began to repattern ourselves, fusing into networks, clusters, and diverse units of social life. We reached beyond ourselves into the seemingly barren environment of outer space to find new life, new resources, new energy, and new knowledge born as a living body . . . opening our eyes into a Universe full of life and light.

Then, as suddenly as it all had begun, the Technicolor movie of creation stopped. I found myself upon the frosty hill in Lakeville, Connecticut—alone. There was no sign of what had happened, yet I knew it had been real. The experience was forever imprinted upon my very cells.

(The End of Barbara's Notes,
Writings, and Journal Entries
on the Planetary Birth Revelation)

Sharing her insights and experience with Earl in breakfast dialogues, a whole new philosophy, and even theology, began to form in Barbara's mind. It sprang from her evolutionary perspective that sees God, Spirit, Consciousness, and the Pattern That Connects as a dynamic consciousness. It is a force creating atoms, molecules, cells, animals, humans—and now breaking through in our consciousness as our *motivation to create,* "as we go around our turn on the spiral," as Barbara put it.

She began to envision a new politics, a new economic system, a new form of education, new energy systems, new governmental and management systems—all are beginning to shift from Earthbound, self-conscious humanity toward universal, whole-centered evolutionary humanity.

Barbara understood now, more than ever, that old systems were breaking down and new systems were breaking through. "All of this is natural but dangerous, just like birth," she told Earl.

"The difference here is that we've never seen another planet go through its transition from its high-tech, overpopulating polluting phase to its potential universal future in harmony with nature and Spirit. Yet the design of creation *must* be for us to awaken within ourselves the capacity to make this shift, both internally as people and socially as a species.

"I felt in my vision that this design is *encoded* in our body/mind; and emulation, peak experiences, and evolutionary ideas trigger it. When 'it' turns on within us, we move from *self-development* to *self-evolution,* from trying to adjust and succeed to a place where we begin to activate inherent and dormant potentials.

"I viewed the great tasks before us with exhilaration and saw our problems as evolutionary drivers. The potential of our new power is to fulfill the deepest aspiration in the human heart for a higher way of life, a greater consciousness, and more freedom."

Over the next few years, Barbara became what she called a "potentialist"—not an optimist or a pessimist. She continued to dialogue with her husband every day.

"I see the emerging pattern and feel completely galvanized toward evolutionary action," she told him one day. "I feel like a new mother with a newborn child. This vision of the conscious evolution of our species has triggered my own evolution."

At another point during her morning breakfasts, she said to Earl, "Darling, this idea liberates more potential and more loving energy than any other idea I have ever experienced."

He smiled. "I'm glad. I'm happy for you."

He didn't get it.

He missed the clue.

🌾 🌾 🌾

REFLECTIONS & EXPLORATIONS

Moving from the Mind to the Soul

As we reflect on the times just described, and look more closely at Barbara's experience to see what we all might benefit from, we are reminded that . . .

> **. . . our connection with the Divine is meant
> to bring us insights and information that the
> Mind itself cannot contain, for it has no previous
> reference point from which to access the data.**

Only the Soul can know what the Mind can barely conceive. Yet how does one access the Soul? Ah, that is the question . . . isn't it?

It is the *Spirit* that acts as a bridge between the Mind and Soul. The Spirit is the Energy of God in Us. This energy can fuel the engine of our experience, taking us wherever it is we wish to go. If we wish to go to higher planes, it can take us there. If we wish to go to the highest planes, it can take us there. This energy—which is Life itself in its more glorious form—can carry us to the peak. Or in Barbara's case, to a hilltop in Connecticut, a mountaintop in California, or the highest place within her own consciousness.

The word *consciousness* should not be construed to mean a space of the Mind. Our consciousness is the *sum total* of what

224

is contained in the Heart, Mind, and Soul. Because it is, truly, *everything*—every awareness, thought, idea, and belief ever held by every sentient being (and by the Source of Sentience itself)—we can access consciousness at many levels. We can enter on the ground floor, climb the stairs to an upper level, float out a window, rise like a balloon, and glide back in an opening at the highest level. We can also fall back out the opening or down the stairs to a lower level again. Where we reside in consciousness depends on where we place our attention.

It is *attention* that keeps us glued to a particular place in consciousness.

I believe that when you are "in your Mind," you are at the lowest level of consciousness, which is all right. That is not an indictment. This is just where you are. Most of the human race is in its Mind most of the time. Even avatars and masters can forget themselves and reside there. ("Father, why hast Thou forsaken me?") The trick, then, is to get out of your head and into your heart.

I often say that to live in this way, you have to be "out of your mind."

The Heart is where the Spirit is stored. What I am calling Spirit is the energy that some others call Love. It is the very energy that animates the Heart at birth—and which leaves the Heart to express an even greater love at death. It is, I'll say again, the Energy of God in Us.

We can use this Energy as fuel with which to travel to the Soul, receiving there all the wisdom, insight, and awareness that the finite Mind (magnificent as it is) cannot contain. This is what happens when we have a vision or a spiritual encounter. This is what happens when we open a channel for continuing dialogue with our Highest Self. We literally connect with the part of us that is a Universal Self, the part of us that *never disconnected* from The All. It is the part of us that is who we really are.

Embracing who we really are requires a change of identity. Now we get to the crux of the "mystery story" that we have been talking about since this book began.

Here is the mystery: *Who am I? Where am I? Why am I here? What can I do about that?*

As in so many mystery stories, we find ourselves involved in *a case of mistaken identity*. Like a person with amnesia, we don't know who we are, yet our lives are designed perfectly to reveal the mystery.

You will see—as you venture even farther back in time in Barbara's life—that her life was exquisitely designed to unveil the mystery for her. And if you look carefully at her life, you will see that, as in all mystery stories, "only the names have been changed to protect the innocent."

We are *all* innocent, and only the names have been changed from one person's story to the next. The roles that are played are always the same. There is the hero and the villain, the protagonist and the antagonist. There is the teacher and the student, the master and the servant, the rich and the poor, the powerful and the powerless. There is the big and the small, the black and the white, the gay and the straight, the liberal and the conservative. And, as the Bible says, "Male and female created He them."

We've changed the names to protect us from our own self-judgment and attacks on others who *are* our very selves—judgments and attacks that grow out of our frustration at not being able to *express* who we deeply *know ourselves to be.*

Once we unravel the Final Mystery of who we all are on this planet, life on the planet itself will change forever. We will, truly, have birthed ourselves into the cosmic community of Universal Beings.

Yet entire life identities don't change overnight (unless they do), and they don't change without reason (unless that is how it happens). Barring the sort of "lightning bolt" experience I talked about in my Reflections following Chapter 15 of this book, identity changes and massive shifts in consciousness producing major life alterations generally follow a long series of events that we would call, loosely, our *life so far.*

It is important to know that the series of events, that life, is not an unconnected string of random occurrences, having neither rhyme nor reason, plan nor purpose, destination nor design. That string of occurrences—*from birth till death*—is the Soul's way of leading you, one step, one situation, one condition, and one circumstance at a time to your next best opportunity to express and fulfill, experience and become, Who You Really Are.

All of which is a long way of saying that nothing—*nothing*—occurs by chance.

This does not mean that your life is predetermined or predestined. It does mean that life's process is so sophisticated, so intricate and complex, that it can and does react and respond moment by moment—in the moment—to the *free choices* that each of us makes, adjusting every nanosecond to guarantee that you stay on course and keep open at all times the opportunity to do what you came here to do.

This may not be apparent to you as you live your life, but it can become increasingly obvious as you look *back* on it, seeing how situations and conditions from your *birth until right now* have served the next step on your journey.

In Barbara's case, the next step on the journey (although she could not know it at the time) was her first significant spiritual encounter: the coming to an awareness of humanity's evolutionary process as the birthing of a planet into the cosmic community of Universal Beings.

Yet she could never have been ready—in a way that Barbara, as a deep situational thinker and an undeclared cosmologist needed to be ready—to receive this remarkable revelation unless she had taken the necessary steps. You do not tell a child where babies come from without first answering for the child other, preparatory, questions. Barbara would never have been equipped to receive a major spiritual revelation—much less ready to undertake the total change of personal identity and purpose that it eventuated —had she not had some preparatory questions answered. And she would not have even *asked* those questions had she not felt the deep unrest that gave their asking both motivation and context.

This is how life works.

I am suggesting to you that *your life* works in *precisely the same way.*

We will explore this truth deeply on the pages ahead, through the telling of more and more of Barbara's story.

Enjoy.

🖉 🖉 🖉

29.

EPISODE #5: DISCOVERY AND LIBERATION, 1960–1965—
the Years Before the Birth Revelation . . .

By 1960, Barbara had turned 30 and was pregnant with her fifth child. She seemed to be falling deeper and deeper asleep during the early months of the 1960s, even while the rest of the human race appeared to be waking up.

It was the time of the flower child and of sexual liberation; of new music (*The Beatles!*); consciousness expansion; and the awakening of the environmental movement, human rights, civil rights, the women's movement, the peace movement, the human-potential movement, the Apollo program . . .

A large chunk of humanity was beginning to see itself as one body. Something new was breaking through, and the energy was being felt even in Lakeville—even in tiny, peaceful, don't-rock-the-boat *Lakeville, Connecticut.*

Barbara, of course, was not living in a cave. Always an astute observer, she was aware of what was going on; and all of this energy movement seemed to snap her out of her malaise. She began to reach out for new life, reading intensively again as she had done in college, searching for ideas that could liberate and guide her.

"Now, not only did I need guidance for greater meaning, but as a mother, I wanted to have something to give to my children besides comfort and caretaking," she reflected later. "Motherhood expanded into the desire to offer my children a glimpse of the deeper purpose of life itself."

The Marx household that Barbara grew up in was Jewish, but her father, Louis, was agnostic. Not having been raised within a traditional religion, Barbara was on her own if she wanted some deeper understanding of life's purpose, promise, and potential—which she definitely did. So she turned once more to books, spending the first years of the decade scouring everything she could find that addressed the larger questions of existence. It was good that she did, because, as she put it: "Major thinkers saved my life."

These included Betty Friedan, author of *The Feminine Mystique;* Abraham Maslow, who wrote *Toward a Psychology of Being;* and Pierre Teilhard de Chardin, whose monumental work *The Phenomenon of Man* may have impacted her the most.

What They Said That Changed Everything

Friedan described how women had this "problem." They seemed to want an identity beyond wife and mother! She called this desire for identity "the feminine mystique." Barbara realized that she had this desire—and, in a sign of the times, the local Freudian psychiatrist with whom she talked about her occasional light depression had called her "neurotic" for longing for more life. Barbara knew that she didn't fit the doctor's label, but she had no immediate answer for it.

In his psychological work, Maslow studied people who were well rather than those who were ill. In reading his work, Barbara learned that Maslow had identified one trait that all truly vibrant people had in common: chosen work they found intrinsically self-rewarding and of service to at least one other.

That was it! Barbara thought. *I am not sick—I am underdeveloped.* Much as she adored her children and husband, motherhood was not her vocation. *It never had been.* It had nothing to do with her "soul's code" or her deep life purpose.

Our motivations for greater purpose are not neurotic; they are essential to our health, she told herself. *We'll get sick, addicted, violent, or depressed if we don't express our higher potential.* People are psychologically *wired* for creative service, she realized. They *can't* be "happy" when they feel selfish or have no purpose that motivates them.

And so, the search was on. It was a quest for life purpose. She remarked: "I put a 'plus sign' on my depression and realized it was not a sign of neurosis but *a vital signal in my awakening.*"

Maslow added something else to Barbara's clarity. He said that there are two ways in which most people find vocation and become self-actualizing:

1. They find someone they admire and wish to emulate who, in turn, recognizes who they really are.

2. They have peak or mystical experiences that transcend the self-conscious mind and help them make the transition from Deficiency-Need Motivation to Growth-Need Motivation. That is, to be *attracted by intrinsic values* rather than *pushed from behind by necessity.*

Maslow mapped the self-actualizing person, and his maps helped create the human-potential movement, giving people something to aim toward that attracted them. "Now there are millions pursuing and experiencing some form of self-actualization," Barbara observes.

Teilhard de Chardin was a Jesuit paleontologist and philosopher whose work was not published by the church in his lifetime. Observing the impact of his writing on her life, Barbara disclosed: "He saw God in evolution. Evolution, he said, is the expression of a Divine process. He found a *pattern* in the process of creation. He saw this as the larger purpose of evolution itself. He called it the Law of complexity/consciousness.

"According to this law, as systems become more complex, they jump in freedom and consciousness, from molecule to cell to animal to human."

Now, Barbara could see that "the *planet itself* is becoming more complex. Everything is linking together through 'globalization.' Each of us is a living member of this living planet."

Barbara embraced his notion that at some point "the connection among us will be so great that we will link heart with heart, center with center, in a mass experience of love and resonance as one living body. A jump in our own consciousness and freedom is possible and, indeed, natural."

Teilhard de Chardin called it *Omega*, Barbara explained, or the *Omega Point*. "He said that humans are about to awaken together in the mind sphere, in consciousness and in capacities. He saw that we would be connected in a living system far greater than the sum of our parts. He saw it as the next stage of our evolution."

Barbara described the overall philosophy as "a form of *evolutionary spirituality*, transcending the materialistic scientific view of evolution as purposeless, mindless, and meaningless, or the idea that an external deity is doing it all to us and for us." Evolution, for Teilhard, she said, "was the expression of Spirit in action for the purpose of creating beings ever more conscious of Spirit."

Bull's-eye

It is difficult to overstate the immense impact that all of this had on a certain diminutive housewife from Connecticut.

"Through Teilhard, my passion for something great coming was affirmed, even as with Maslow, my desire for purpose was affirmed," she wrote in her notes later.

"I began to 'turn on' to my own creativity. I experienced the early phase of 'vocational arousal.' The treasure hunt for vocation was getting hotter. I was close to discovery. I woke up charged with excitement. This is how you can tell that you're on the developmental path!"

And as if that wasn't enough, she found another great thinker to inspire her: American architect, designer, inventor, author, and futurist Buckminster Fuller. She was intrigued by his famous statement that "Spaceship Earth came without an Operating Manual," and overjoyed when she read his assessment that humans now held the resources, technology, and know-how to make of this world a 100 percent physical success for all people.

For Barbara, it all began to fit together. She wrote in her journal: "The purpose of our new powers is to actualize unique human potential as part of a spiritual evolution toward oneness and love, with the technological and social capacity to free all people to do and be their best in a universe of immeasurable resources and dimensions."

Putting her pen down, she sat back and read what she'd just entered.

There it is, she thought, *from Maslow, Friedan, Teilhard de Chardin, Buckminster Fuller . . . the answer to the question that not even the President of the United States could answer. Wait until everyone hears this!*

The Result of Being "Seen"

Barbara was filled with all of this reading. Yet she was still the housewife in Lakeville, Connecticut; still without an understanding of her own depression, her own intuition of something more coming.

One beautiful fall day in 1964, she was sitting with her children in the golden sunlight of the New England autumn, the trees shimmering, the grass a vivid green, when the phone rang. She went inside and picked it up.

"Mrs. Hubbard?"

"Yes . . ."

"This is Jonas Salk."

"*Doctor* Jonas Salk?" Barbara could not believe her ears.

"Well, yes," he said modestly. The world-renowned creator of the Salk vaccine was, indeed, on the other end of the line. He had brought a virtual end to the most frightening public health problem of the postwar United States—polio—and had founded the Salk Institute for Biological Studies in La Jolla, California.

He was also a futurist of the first rank, and a lookup on Wikipedia reveals that he anxiously anticipated the eventual appearance of what he described as "a new and important school of thinkers" who would include those who recognize that humans are not only the product of the process of evolution, but that *we have become the process itself,* through the emergence and evolution of our consciousness, our awareness, our capacity to imagine and anticipate the future, and to choose from among alternatives."

This, of course, lined up perfectly with Barbara's ideas. Yet this global figure would not have ever contacted Barbara had it not been for the fact that she had written a letter to the editor of *Scientific American* containing her thoughts and vision about an idea Salk had about creating a Theater of Man. (Barbara preaches that this is one of the key factors for evolutionaries. "It is vital to be bold enough to follow the compass of joy, to find, to contact whatever most attracts you," she often says.)

"You have stated my dream of the Theater of Man better than I could," Dr. Salk told her. We are two peas in the same genetic pod. I would very much like to speak further with you, and I will be in New York soon. May I invite you to lunch?"

"Yes," Barbara replied breathlessly, and they set a date and time. Hanging up, she returned to her children—but something had happened. A new voice had reached her, something she had never felt before. She waited for the day he would pick her up with barely contained joy. It was the phrase "two peas in the same genetic pod," that stayed with her. What did this mean?

The day arrived. The doorbell rang. Barbara opened the door, and there he was. Instant attraction flooded. He looked around at her apple orchard where she had sat for endless hours writing in her journal and asking for greater meaning in life.

"This is beautiful," he said. "This is like the Garden of Eden."

"Yes," she agreed, smiling. "And I'm Eve . . . and I'm leaving!"

As they drove to a restaurant in the city, tears were flowing down her face. She pretended to have a bad case of hay fever. All the way to New York, she told him about the things that were "wrong" with her . . . she was attracted to the future, she felt something great was coming, she wanted to participate more fully, she yearned to reach out and connect with others of like mind.

"Barbara," he remarked, "this is not what is wrong with you— this is what is right with you. You are a psychological mutant. You combine the characteristics needed by evolution now."

This simple sentenced changed her life.

She told him how she had read in Teilhard's writings that a new kind of human was evolving, a kind that had been inspired by the ideas of evolution. He called this type "Homo progressivus," someone in whom "the flame of expectation burns," who has a "mysterious sense of the future as an organism progressing toward the unknown."

She explained to Jonas Salk that Teilhard de Chardin felt that this type would eventually gain dominion over Earth because these individuals got more and more energy through their attraction to the future; while another type of human he called "the bourgeois," wanted to control life and hold on to it as it is. The latter type, Teilhard noted, would be ever more stressed, because life *cannot* be controlled.

Barbara continued: "Jonas, Teilhard said that if he met even one person like that in a room, nothing on Earth could keep them separated."

"It's true," he said, "and I will introduce you to the few others I've met in 25 years of searching."

Jonas's recognition of Barbara's Essential Self fit the exact experience profile that she had read about in Maslow's writing—that individuals become self-actualizing when they find someone they admire and wish to emulate who, in turn, recognizes who they really are. Jonas awakened Barbara's evolutionary nature. Instead of remaining a discontent housewife in Lakeville, she became an evolutionary woman. The process of liberation had begun.

A Second Enormous Influence

Then came a nearly identical experience with Abraham Maslow himself.

After reading his book *Toward a Psychology of Being* (learning about self-actualizing humans, and yearning to be one herself), she followed his suggestion to reach out to what attracts you. Barbara found out how to reach him, called him, and said, "Dr. Maslow, your book has saved my life. Will you come to lunch?"

Amazingly, he said *yes*.

(This is another example for evolutionaries: *Be bold! Reach out!*)

Maslow came to her New York apartment, and she told him about her passion to find out what is good, what is evolving, and where the human race is going. He was inspired.

"Barbara," he said, "all my life I have been rejected by others in my field for seeking out what is growing and good in the human personality. . . . But I've made a list of the good souls, the 'eupsychian network' of people like us who are attracted to what's emerging in themselves and others. I have a list of 300 names, which I will give to you." (This was before the human-potential movement had even been labeled.)

Barbara took the names and began to network. Several years later, she wrote "The Center Letter," a mimeographed sheet that she sent to everyone on Maslow's list, as well as to those on Jonas Salk's list, and to other people she had simply read about. The letter said that she wanted to know what each of these leaders felt was the next step for the human good. She promised to publish excerpts of their answers. She mailed the letters from the old post office in Lime Rock, Connecticut. And waited. Would anybody respond?

Within a few weeks, the letters started to come in from all over the world. (This was way, way before e-mail!) Fr. Thomas Merton wrote back, and so did Willis Harman and Lewis Mumford. . . .

Barbara published *The Center Letter* for several years. It made its way throughout the world, people sharing it with others. *Homo progressivus* responded. She was no longer alone. Suddenly she was connected, vitalized, animated, transforming.

One Element Still Missing

But before *The Center Letter,* Barbara had only met Jonas Salk, Abe Maslow, and a few others Jonas introduced her to. Those meetings (while they were inspirational for sure, and did so much for her in terms of discovery and liberation) didn't give her the insights she needed to incorporate or integrate all these great ideas into her own body/mind. More important, she didn't know what her true part or calling in all of this *was.* She was overflowing with ideas, aspirations, and excitement, but had very little *clarity* about what to *do* about them.

And while Barbara had asked tons of people, whose opinion she deeply respected, the question: "What is the next step for the human good?" she still had no insight about humanity's Larger Story.

Then . . . she went for an afternoon walk up a hill near her Connecticut home in the frigid temperature of a February afternoon in 1966, and it happened. She was given a vision of the Planetary Birth Experience, and with it, her vocation: *Go tell the story of our birth!*

30.

EPISODE #4: QUESTION FOR A PRESIDENT, 1953—
Seven Years Before the Discovery and Liberation . . .

Sometimes it's the shortest moments that create the longest impact. And sometimes it's the most "I had nothing to do with it" facts of our life that have the most to do with what we *are* doing with our life.

Did you get that? I know that it's a rather convoluted collection of words, but read it again if you didn't pick up on it, because I really would like you to "get" that.

It was not lost on me as I delved deeper and deeper into Barbara Marx Hubbard's life that all of the dominoes were set up in perfect alignment to fall in perfect sequence once the first one toppled. Let's call the first domino her birth. Everything after that lines up magnificently with logical appearance on her 83rd birthday, as the principal public figure at the Day One event on December 22, 2012.

The entirety of Barbara's life, including that moment in 2012, has been animated by a single question. But it wasn't something she asked of just anyone. Rather, she asked those whom *she fully expected would have an answer.* And when a particular person she queried didn't, the moment stuck with her for the rest of her life.

She sensed that it was important that he *did* have an answer. She very much felt that he *should* have had an answer. Yet he did not. *And if he doesn't have an answer,* Barbara asked herself, *who does?*

The Dominoes Start to Tumble

Barbara's question was asked of the President of the United States, standing in his office.

To understand how this young woman even found herself in a position to pose such an inquiry of such a person in such a place, we need to know a little more about Barbara's family of origin.

Barbara's life was perfectly "designed" from its beginning and redesigned with perfection at every step along the way. The backward look that this book has taken has made that very clear to me.

As a little girl, there was nothing Barbara really wanted that she could not have. Her father was Louis Marx, the creator of the biggest toy company in America—and arguably, in the world. Born in Brooklyn, he built his empire, his own life, from the ground up. There was certainly nothing lacking in the Marx household . . . especially not *toys.* Louis actually brought home tons of toys then in development by his company, as well as competitors' toys, and would anxiously watch his children to see how they reacted to them. Would other children like them, too? Did he have another winner? Which toys did his kids like best?

As might be expected, Barbara went to the best schools, eventually attending Bryn Mawr College outside Philadelphia. She spent her junior year abroad in Paris; and like something straight out of a movie, she fell in love with a disaffected, earnest, handsome, young American artist who happened to join her at a tiny table in a smoke-filled coffee shop tucked away on some side street. She returned with him to the States, had a fairy-tale wedding, and settled down to become the model 1950s wife and mother.

Now don't get me wrong. There were some difficult moments along the way in Barbara's life. An early preteen tragedy produced deep anger toward God, and a later teenage perplexity produced deep questioning *about* life. But for the most part, and as childhoods in the aftermath of the American Depression went, Barbara had a pretty doggone good go of it.

The only problem was that the deep anger she had was never expressed, and those deep questions were never answered. . . .

Taking Her Question to the Top

Over the years, Louis Marx had occasion to meet many interesting people—included among them not a few military generals. That happened because Bernard Gimbel, a powerful New York businessman, had brought General Hap Arnold of the Air Force to Louis's office to see if his factory might have a part of a missing toy train that Arnold had lost. Louis had someone locate it on the workroom floor, and he gave it to the general. The two became friends, and through him, Louis befriended other generals—including Dwight Eisenhower, who would later, of course, become President of the United States.

By 1952, Louis had remarried and eventually had five new sons. Each had a general as a godfather. And so it came to pass, just after Eisenhower was elected President, that there was a family meeting planned at Gen. Omar Bradley's home to take a picture of the generals and the President with their godsons. Gen. Omar Bradley, Gen. George C. Marshall, Gen. Rosie O'Donnell, and Gen. Walter Bedell Smith were all there; along with various aunts and uncles and members of the Marx family: Barbara's sisters Patricia and Jacqueline, and brother Louis, Jr.

Not long after that event, Barbara was invited to make a courtesy call on the President in the White House.

At the appointed hour, she and her father were ushered into the Oval Office, located in the southeast corner of the huge mansion on Pennsylvania Avenue. The President was on his feet and put his hand out to Barbara's father. "Louis, it's always good to see you," he said congenially, and he meant it. "Please, sit down." The three of them moved to the facing couches that stood a few feet from the Chief Executive's desk.

Dwight Eisenhower and Louis Marx then entered into a discussion about the growing power of the military/industrial complex. "It's not something to take lightly, Louis," the President said.

"I know," Barbara's father replied. "There's an awful lot of power there."

Barbara shifted her weight, drawing Eisenhower's attention. He picked up on her silent signal that she had something she wished to say. "What can I do for you, young lady?" he asked kindly.

"Mr. President, I have a question for you," she said.

"And what is that, my dear?"

"You and Father spoke just now about our awesome power."

"Yes."

Looking into his brilliant blue eyes, she was, for an instant, speechless . . . magnetized. But only for an instant. Then Barbara Marx Hubbard asked President Dwight David Eisenhower: "What is the meaning of our new power that is good?"

Not What She Expected

The President appeared startled, glanced at Louis, and then looked back to Barbara and shook his head. His voice sounded sad, almost depleted. Then, slowly, he replied: "I do not know. I have no idea. . . ."

The thought occurred to Barbara: *Well, then, we had better find out!* But she didn't say that to the President. She simply sat quietly, respectfully, and smiled.

"Your daughter seems to have asked the question of the century," President Eisenhower ruefully noted to Louis.

"Yes, well . . . she has a way of doing that," Barbara's father remarked and chuckled.

It was Barbara's turn to be startled. She didn't know what kind of answer to expect from the former war hero and five-star general —who knew all about the exercise of power—but she had hoped for *some* sort of answer.

This little incident turned out to be not really a "little incident" at all, for it fueled the experience of Barbara Marx Hubbard for the better part of her life thereafter. Although it was true that the drive to find out the purpose of our power and what she was meant to do diminished when she was pregnant, which seemed to be her condition almost constantly over the next few years. Within six years of that White House visit, she was to have four children. By 1960, she would have one more.

Barbara was a devoted mother, remaining at home full-time, and was deeply in love with her husband and every one of the beautiful little beings she and Earl had brought into the world.

Yet a longing for more life, and the lack of an answer to her life's major question, pressed upon her. Her children would say years later that they knew she loved them, but they felt that she was often not fully "there."

"They were right," Barbara told me. "Even though the children were the love of my life, I was such a passionate seeker, that my deepest attention was always elsewhere, searching for the purpose and direction of life."

Interestingly, what led her to this place of distraction and ennui was something that she had imagined would do *exactly the opposite.*

🐾 🐾 🐾

EPISODE #3: LOVE, MARRIAGE, AND CHILDREN, 1949—
Four Years Prior to the Question for a President . . .

Barbara had begun keeping a journal since May 27, 1948, when she was 18 years old. Rarely have many days gone by when she hasn't written something in it. And certainly, no major event in her life has escaped her written attention.

She has all of those journal pages to this day, which makes it easy for someone who wants to track her life backward. Very few of us can remember all the things that have happened to us in our earliest years—much less all the things we *said* or even *thought*. With Barbara, the challenge has not been insufficient material, but almost *too much*.

Still, it's been delightful to browse through many of her personal notes and recollections—the majority of which have never been seen by anyone, and a few of which have made their way to previously published, but not widely read, material. There's nothing like written accounts when it comes to descriptions of some of someone's most memorable moments. . . .

A Parisian Encounter

It was a rainy November afternoon in 1949. Barbara had been living in Paris since late summer, having left the United States for a year to attend classes at the Sorbonne and the École des Sciences Politiques. She had been looking for something she couldn't find at Bryn Mawr, but what she wound up finding was something she hadn't found anywhere: a man she could fall in love with.

Barbara was always around other students in those days; and, in fact, this November day was the very first time since she'd arrived in France that she had lunched alone.

It was a coincidence. Yes (*ahem*), another sheer coincidence. There is no plan here, no design, no intricate tapestry . . . right?

Riiiight . . .

So here is Barbara, having her first lunch alone in Paris, *ever,* in a tiny little restaurant on the Left Bank called Chez Rosalie.

The place is jammed, and there is only one small round table left, with a chair on each side. Barbara takes it, sits down, and orders a small beef steak and a half bottle of red wine. She is not yet 21, but in Paris, who cares? No one bothers to ask her age.

Soon, the door swings open. Shall we let Barbara describe her first glimpse of her future husband?

A Woman's Fond Memory . . .

"A tall young man entered. He had a large aristocratic head, with thick, curly, dark hair and full lips. He was gaunt, with hollows at his cheekbones. I noticed his long, thin fingers as he took off his duffle coat and hung it on the rack. His presence struck me like an electric shock. In a moment, his eyes scanned the room and caught mine. I smiled and lowered my head, knowing he would have to sit opposite me. It was the only place available."

He sauntered over, sat down, and they exchanged pleasantries. The two smiled. They were going to get along—that was clear. "I'm Earl Hubbard."

"Hello. I'm Barbara Marx."

Barbara told Earl that she was interested in the meaning of life. Then she went for the jugular with her perennial—and usually disqualifying—question: "What is your purpose?"

Earl didn't blink.

"I'm an artist. My purpose is to create a new image of man commensurate with our capacities to shape the future."

Barbara could hardly believe her ears. She wrote later: "Instantaneously, the idea flashed through my mind: *I'm going to marry him.* I smiled radiantly and nodded my head. Tears came to my eyes."

And that was that. We could make a longer story out of this, because there are a lot of details that could be filled in about the time between that November afternoon and the January day 14 months later when the two met at the altar at Saint Thomas Church in New York City and became man and wife. But those details are not really important to this story.

Of Refrigerators and Dryers

What is important is what happened in the years afterward. Barbara returned to Bryn Mawr to graduate—pregnant. After her first child, Suzanne, was born, she settled in to a life very much unlike what she thought she was getting into when she sat across from that exciting intellectual in Paris.

She and Earl had found a small studio in Lime Rock, Connecticut. They could have lived anywhere had Earl been okay with Barbara helping out financially with her income from her father, but he was having none of it. It was his job, he said, to support his wife; and they could do with what money he could provide.

Barbara found this bit of male pride a bit amusing since Earl was living as an artist on money from *his* father, but she let it rest and allowed her husband to have his way. *In almost everything.* For instance, Barbara had wanted to live in Washington, D.C., where she knew her father had many connections, and where she might find a job working with or for somebody in a way that could help her activate her real purpose. But Earl wanted to be alone, living the life of an isolated artist. And he wanted his wife to stay at home—not be a working mother. Like her mother before her, when faced with the choices and decisions of Louis, Barbara acquiesced. So there they were, hanging out in a tiny studio in Lime Rock.

"I entered a period of trying to make a home for my daughter and husband," her writings in later years tell us. "It became perfectly obvious that—as much as I didn't want to—I would have to concern myself with stoves, dryers, washing machines, and refrigerators. I had thought I was getting out of the material world when I married a man of high purpose, but because I had a baby and because it was Earl's desire, I got deeper into it."

Barbara was changing from a witty, charming, literate conversationalist and observer of life who wanted to continue discovering and learning more and more (and then find her own life purpose and follow it), to a diminutive wife and mother in a tiny studio apartment making breakfast, straightening up the place, bathing and feeding and playing with her baby, lying in the sun, playing a little piano, writing in her journal, taking a walk, making dinner, cleaning up the dishes, reading, listening to the radio, and going to sleep. In a word, she was bored. In three words, she was *bored to tears.*

Barbara noticed a difference in Earl, too. A big difference.

"The social, witty, philosophical young man I had met in Paris who painted charming paintings of French scenes as gifts for his friends, who conversed for hours in cafés, suddenly changed upon marriage to me," she wrote. "He became intense, seeking isolation and craving affirmation of his work."

The remainder of the 1950s was, for Barbara, a time that felt almost surreal. "It was the strange experience of loving and caring for my family while at the same time feeling lost . . . depressed," was the way she described it. "I felt incarcerated within myself, like I was turning to stone. Something in me was dying to be born. I found out later that it was my Self."

🐾 🐾 🐾

Mistakes Are Not Possible

As we reflect on the times just described, and look more closely at Barbara's experience to see what we all might benefit from, we are reminded that . . .

> **. . . there is no such thing as a "wrong turn" on the road of Life. An Intelligence far greater than that of the Mind is at work in the continuing mapping of our lives.**

The questions that we must ask now are: *Was this all a "mistake"? Was Barbara's decision to marry Earl Hubbard, have five children, and settle into "regular married life" in the '50s in a village in Connecticut a derailing? Did these events get her <u>off track,</u> or did they actually set her <u>on track,</u> in the most impactful and profound way?*

It is important to recall what we said earlier here: We always have Free Will, and nothing in life is predestined. Our Soul has laid out a map, yes, but we are not required to follow it.

It is not actually a "map" so much as one of those GPS devices that we now see in cars. You punch in where you want to go and the satellite positioning device tells you exactly how to get there. *But you don't have to follow any particular route.* Whatever route you choose, whatever decision you make, the GPS simply makes an *instant adjustment,* instantly creating a new way to get to where you want to go *from where you are now.* The Soul makes these kinds of "path adjustments" by the nanosecond.

In that sense, there is no way you can get lost. And in that sense, *no way is the "wrong way" to where you want to go.*

With the foolproof device of the Soul's Knowing, we all wind up back Home with God in a Life That Never Ends—having experienced exactly what we wanted to as evinced by the fact that *we experienced it.*

So . . . were Barbara's marriage and children a "mistake"? Absolutely not. The moment she made those freewill decisions, her interior "global positioning device" built them into her journey and showed her how to *use them perfectly* to get her to where she wanted to go.

It is arguable, in fact, that these decisions *fueled and expedited* her return to the search for answers to life's larger questions, including the Big Question of 1945. Had she not found herself in a space of such internal frustration, she might have blithely moved forward with her life, assuming the questions of her youth to have been just that: the simplistic inquiries of an immature mind caught up in fashionable, but not terribly meaningful, intellectualisms.

Only after settling into adult life *as it was being lived* by so many people could she see how huge swaths of humanity, herself included, had been caught up in day-to-day entanglements that they began to make very real and very important . . . but that had nothing at all to do with the larger purpose of our existence or the solutions to the biggest problems and challenges facing our species.

It was the *yearning* for the answers to life's larger questions that was being intensified for Barbara. And it seems clear that a deep and rich experience of *motherhood* was going to be necessary for her to find, really hear, fully embrace, and magnificently *tell* humanity's New Story.

Could a person who had never been a mother and who had never experienced the deep, rich, cellular impulse to both produce life—and to protect and nurture it—ever have internalized the Birth Story as completely as Barbara did?

Yet would the yearning for answers to life's larger questions even be present in order to *be* intensified had nothing stimulated such questions to begin with? Many people, after all, go through their entire lives without posing such queries (much less to other people). Yet what if there *was* a plan? What if it was Barbara's purpose to not only ask, but also to answer the questions that the whole world had been asking? What if Barbara was to be a catalyst —one among many—who would openly and *publicly* ask life's biggest questions . . . and then propose answers that the world would be invited to discuss?

In order for this to happen, something major, something big, something really important and meaningful, would have to occur that would ignite a deep and very real need to ask life's largest questions.

We will explore this truth deeply on the pages ahead, through the telling of more and more of Barbara's story.

Enjoy.

ℓ ℓ ℓ

32.

EPISODE #2: THE EARLIEST QUESTIONS, 1943—
Six Years Before Love, Marriage, and Children . . .

Rene Marx was beautiful. It was as simple as that. She was stunning in a gauzy sort of way, like a movie star in an old black-and-white film where the leading lady is never seen in sharp focus.

She was also sweet, gentle, kind, loving, deeply caring, and completely submissive to her husband, Louis. When she moved, she moved easily, as if gliding. When she spoke, she spoke softly, hovering just above a whisper. And when she gave her children her personal attention, a little hug or a good-night kiss, all was well with the world. Barbara and her siblings—her brother, Louis, and sisters, Patricia and Jacqueline—felt utterly safe.

Barbara's father adored her, and she felt secure in his love. In many ways, she was living a fantasy existence. The Marx apartment in New York City was spacious and beautiful. The toy closet overflowed. Barbara enjoyed the fun of sledding with her brother and sisters in Central Park, the excitement of being taken to opening nights on Broadway, and the laziness of summer days on a farm in Connecticut. She attended The Dalton School and was given the best of everything.

And then, when she was 12, her mother died. Cruelly, devastatingly, Rene's life abruptly ended. And Barbara's childhood was over.

Rene had been ill for more than year. It was breast cancer, and Barbara was old enough to know just how serious that was, but somewhere deep within, she thought that her mother would survive. Barbara had not been raised in a religious household, but she knew that there was this thing called "God," Who, some said, ran the show down here. She didn't know exactly how to do it, but she tried as best she could to pray hard during that year of her mother's illness.

"Please, God," she would whisper, "make Mom better. *Make Mom better.* I'll do anything! You can take *me,* but save Mom." She meant it. She was ready to die if her mother could live. She had faith in some power for the good.

Barbara also felt that the family had a Protector Against All Bad Outcomes in her father. Louis Marx was a big man in every way. His voice was big, his body was big, his presence was big—and he smoked that big cigar. He brought mass production to the toy-making industry and soon had a very, very big business. He made big money at Louis Marx and Company, and he had big power. He was close friends with generals, admirals, and other people in high office. So it was natural that Barbara thought her father could fix anything.

He'll get the best doctors! she told herself. *She will be in the best hospital and get the best care. She will get better!* Louis had already moved the family out of their apartment in the city to a mansion in suburban Scarsdale. He wanted to get them all away from that hectic energy, traffic exhaust, and congestion and into a place where there was much more space and where Rene could be better cared for.

Once, between Rene's hospital visits, Barbara accidentally pushed against her mother's bathroom door. She caught a glimpse of the scar on her mother's chest where a breast had been removed. Barbara turned away in horror, but not before catching her mother's eyes and sensing her terror . . . "like a deer caught in the flashlight of a hunter—doomed," Barbara would later write.

Then came the evening when her father sat all the children down in the living room. He'd just come home from the hospital. "Children," he rasped, "little Mother is dead." He swept his offspring in his arms, trying to pull them all onto his lap. Then he buried his face in Barbara's shoulder and wept.

At first Barbara and the others were very quiet . . . but only for the smallest moment, as they took in the shock. Then they sobbed—deep, heaving sobs—as their father comforted them. "It's all right to cry," he said. "There's nothing else to do."

Writing about the moment, Barbara describes a fierce anger suddenly awakening in her, rising out of the despair. A powerful driving force within her said silently: *No! I will not cry. I do not accept death! There is something more, but I've got to find out . . . I can't tolerate this.*

"My mother was innocent," her memoirs go on. "God was unfair. A deep knot of pain lodged itself in my solar plexus. I felt abandoned. I was only 12, but the real hunger for meaning had begun."

A Second Major Moment

Her mother's passing was the first of two events in her early years that made an indelible mark on her psyche, foundationally shaping Barbara's future. The second occurred on August 6, 1945.

In that month, the United States dropped two atomic bombs on Japan.

Barbara, 15, was shocked and horrified. Thousands of people died in an instant. Others were maimed and disfigured for life. Two huge cities were flattened. President Truman and the U.S. government asserted that this carnage was regretfully needed to end the war. Furthermore, they argued, it prevented ten times more casualties of Allied soldiers than if a standard land invasion of the Pacific Islands was used to defeat Japan. Many in America disagreed, however. A report by the Federal Council of Churches titled "Atomic Warfare and the Christian Faith" includes the following passage:

As American Christians, we are deeply penitent for the irresponsible use already made of the atomic bomb. We are agreed that, whatever be one's judgment of the war in principle, the surprise bombings of Hiroshima and Nagasaki are morally indefensible.

Until that day, Barbara had felt that life was good, America was good, and our power was good. Her father had told her so. His motto was: "Do your best. If you work hard, you can get anything, do anything."

"Suddenly, I saw that if we really worked hard, we could destroy everything," Barbara would write later. Her head pounded with the Big Question: *What is the meaning of all this new scientific/technological power that is good?*

There just *had* to be some *good* meaning, some good purpose, or what was the point of going on with life? For that matter, would it even be possible to *do* so, unless our new power was harnessed and refocused for positive outcomes?

Where is our civilization going? Barbara earnestly yearned to know. For a young woman on the edge of adulthood, it was a fair, and a very concerned, question.

She looked everywhere for an answer. She turned to books. She read lots of philosophy and religion, searching for one thing: positive images of the future equal to our new powers—not in life after death, not in some metaphysical dimension, not in some golden age in the past, but life on this earth, in the future.

When she read the New Testament for the first time, there it was: "Behold, I show you a mystery; we shall not all sleep, we shall all be changed, in a moment, in the twinkling of an eye, at the last trump: for the trumpet shall sound."

That spoke to her. *I'll join the church,* she thought. So at 16, she headed to an Episcopal Church in Scarsdale. She met the priest and asked him her questions: "Is any of this true? Did this really happen? Shall we all be changed, and if so, how . . . ?

"When Jesus said that we could do the same works that he did, and even more, what did he mean? Is it true? What about the Resurrection, the Ascension, and the Second Coming? Shall we have new bodies like his? Shall we overcome death?"

And then . . .

"What is the purpose of humanity's awesome power? What is its meaning for *good*?"

The poor priest was overwhelmed. These were more questions (and better ones) than he'd get from his Sunday school class in a month. Unfortunately, he could answer none of them to Barbara's satisfaction. His responses seemed shallow, canned, and delivered as if he himself didn't fully believe them. The priest advised her to attend Sunday school, and she did, also bringing her brother and sisters with her.

One Sunday the priest was telling the story of Genesis: Eve was guilty, she was expelled from the Garden because of her curiosity, her love of knowledge, and she was responsible for the fall of man. Barbara became so distressed that she almost fell out of the pew.

Somewhere within her, a voice arose. *No, we are not guilty,* it said. *I am not guilty!*

Yet the coding of that story began to work in her heart. *Who is the modern Eve?* she asked herself. *What is her true heart's desire now?* Out of this came an entire book *(The Hunger of Eve)* in which Barbara wrote:

> It seemed to me that Jehovah was more at fault than we were. His behavior toward His children was unacceptable. I thought, *Here we are, weak creatures treated cruelly by a God who had all the characteristics of a male tyrant.* I wanted to run up to the priest and start preaching to *him:* "If God is good, and we are created in His image, than we are good, too! We must respect ourselves, not hate ourselves!" But, of course, I couldn't say a word.

Barbara left the church, unable to believe what she was being taught.

Searching for Purpose

Discovering that Bryn Mawr was one of the best and most intellectually challenging of the women's colleges, Barbara chose to go there. She was now not only seeking answers to her life's biggest questions, but also a clear sense of purpose. *Purpose* seemed to dominate her thinking. She wanted to know the purpose of humanity's new power, the purpose of life itself, and her own purpose *in* life. And it all had to tie together—it had to make integrative sense.

But Barbara found little challenge at the school, where there was no inclination at all on the part of her professors to discuss the questions that continued to hold her focus. She would write in her journal about this later: "There seemed no genuine way to search for one's own life purpose, nor to find how that purpose related to the whole society of which I was a part, much less the future of humanity."

Barbara achieved cum laude grades in her studies, but college wasn't helping her learn what she was supposed to do—or anything, really, about *purpose.*

She found the same lack of substance in most of the young men she had begun attracting. She would ask, "What is your purpose? What are you working for?" only to find that none of them had even thought about it.

Against this backdrop, Barbara applied to Sweet Briar College in Virginia for its year-abroad program; and with her good grades, she was immediately accepted. (The college to this day offers several study-abroad programs to its students, the two largest being junior year in France or Spain.)

Barbara chose France. And there, in a tiny little restaurant in Paris called Chez Rosalie, she stopped to have lunch one day. . . .

🌾 🌾 🌾

33.

EPISODE #1: ENTERING THE WORLD, DECEMBER 22, 1929—
Thirteen Years Before the Earliest Questions . . .

Two months prior to the birth of Barbara Marx Hubbard, the United States suffered the most devastating stock-market crash in its history, bringing the so-called Roaring Twenties to a screeching halt and creating a ten-year economic slump of such severity that it was called the Great Depression.

How bad was the crash? Wikipedia, quoting economist Richard Salsman, puts it into context in this way: "Anyone who bought stocks in mid-1929 and held on to them saw most of his or her adult life pass by before getting back to even."

The market lost $14 billion in value on one day alone (October 29, 1929), and $30 billion in a single week.

None of this had much of an effect on Louis Marx and his wife, Rene, however. Rene was pregnant with her first child, and Louis was a self-made man running his own highly successful toy-manufacturing business. He'd become a millionaire by the age of 30. And as the Depression set in, people spent less and less on outside-the-house entertainment for themselves or their children.

That meant they had to spend what little money they had on *inside*-the-house entertainment for their little ones—and *that* meant toys . . . if only someone could find a way to produce them cheaply enough.

Louis Marx already had. Called the "Henry Ford of the toy business," he brought assembly-line efficiency to the making of his toys. Many people could still afford them, and so money continued to pour into Louis Marx and Company.

Entering the World

On December 22, 1929, Barbara was born, a child of the Great Depression utterly unaffected by it. Her earliest years were lived in comfort and splendor—her days passed in the family's Fifth Avenue apartment surrounded by more toys than the average child would see in a lifetime and attended to by a doting mother. When she grew older, she attended the exclusive Dalton School; played the piano; ate chocolate éclairs; and during the hot summer, she had hose fights with her friends on the penthouse, roof, and terrace.

I have not idealized this to make it sound even slightly better than it was. Most of these words are from Barbara's own description, appearing in other writings. Her life was just this side of *fantasy*—and the sad thing about it was that she didn't even know it. She didn't hold a notion of herself as being "happy." She simply thought: *This is the way life is.*

Yet all of us, no matter how wonderful our upbringing, receive imprints that ultimately tell us how life *really* is. It is the way of Life itself, telling us *about* itself. It is how we come to *know* that we are "happy" when we are. Among other things, every child sooner or later receives imprints of fear, guilt, loss, anger, hurt, horror, and hopelessness.

It was no different for Barbara.

Her first encounter with fear and guilt occurred at the same time, when she was six years old and caught a glimpse of the "outside world"—the world as it existed for millions of people during the Depression.

Her father had taken her with him on a drive somewhere in his shiny Rolls-Royce convertible. The car was moving through the streets of New York, and in the neighborhood known as Harlem it stopped at a red light on Second Avenue.

It was a cold, ugly, rainy twilight. Suddenly, appearing seemingly out of nowhere, the Rolls was surrounded by older boys and young men, peering in the windows on all sides, their faces pressed right up against the glass. They were not dressed very well against the chill. Some, in fact, appeared to be in rags. The light seemed to be taking forever to turn green, and the car began to rock. The people on the outside were doing it, Barbara suddenly realized. For the first time in her life, she was scared. She also felt, for the first time, a kind of guilt. *How can I be in this wonderful, warm car with a fur rug on my lap while those men are out there freezing, with little on their backs?* she wondered.

The light finally changed and the car moved on, Barbara tightly squeezing her father's hand under the rug. It was a moment she never forgot, imprinting indelible feelings on her soul, and pressing into her mind vivid images of what it means to "have" and "have not." She felt it was not fair, not right.

More Childhood Imprints

Six years later Barbara received the imprint of loss and anger—also at the same time—when her mother died of breast cancer. Barbara was shocked. How could anyone so perfect, so wonderful, so innocent, so beautiful, die so young? Death was for *old* people—and, frankly, Barbara didn't understand why anyone had to die at all!

Not long after that, she felt the imprint of personal hurt. She was a new student at Rye Country Day School in Rye, New York, outside the city in Westchester County; and none of the students wanted much to do with her. The shunning became really obvious when it came time for the first big school dance of the year. Barbara wasn't invited and didn't understand why. She went around asking, but the other kids just looked at her and said things like, "You don't *know?!*" She didn't, of course, or she wouldn't have asked. Finally, she begged someone to "just tell me the truth!" And so, the other child did: "You will *never* be invited to *anything* here," she sniffed, "because you're *Jewish.*"

Barbara was stunned. She had never run across anything like that at The Dalton School in the city. She never even thought of herself as Jewish. Her father was an agnostic who didn't go to temple, nor had he ever met a rabbi in his life. How could anyone hold her family's way-back-there cultural history against *her?*

Finally, Barbara felt horror and hopelessness when, at 15, she saw the Hearst Metrotone News pictures of the atomic blasts over Japan.

Whatever the judgments of history might be, Barbara's in-the-moment mind—having already collected the data from her frightening moment in Harlem, the crushing loss of her mother's death, and the deeply hurtful experience of prejudice at her school—suddenly flooded with questions, questions, *questions.* . . .

Barbara's birth into a home of privilege created the perfect context within which she could experience the pain of life in a deep way that very few children or young adults would. The urgent questions emerging from that pain gave birth to a life of inquiry—and that lifetime of searching, in turn, gave birth to the new story of humanity's birth itself.

What began on December 22, 1929, came to fruition on December 22, 2012.

From Day One to Day One . . . the circle was complete.

🌿 🌿 🌿

NOTES OF A DETECTIVE

If I can be forgiven a figure of speech, I think it is a "crime" that it has taken me and the rest of humanity so long to truly understand what is going on here. In this life, I mean. At this critical time, I mean.

Even if life is a mystery, it shouldn't take us forever to unravel it. My only hope is that this book has helped move all of us along in that process.

I've come upon the "scene of the crime," so to speak, after a person has "died." It was my job to figure out how Barbara Marx Hubbard lost her life—her old life, that is—and gained *new life* as a new person with a new and glorious identity that reflects the wonder of who we all really are.

We are all, it turns out, living a Case of Mistaken Identity. We do not know who we really are, where we are, or what we are doing here. And that is why life, for most of us, has made no sense at all, leaving us to bumble through it as best we can.

As we reflect a final time on all the Episodes described in this book, and look more closely at Barbara's total life experience to see what we all might benefit from, we are reminded that . . .

. . . the miracle of Life's self-creating design is being played out in every minute of every hour of every day in every way. There is simply no such thing as "chance."

Life works in mysterious ways to produce the wonder, beauty, and *intricacy* of its tapestry. One thread out of place, one weaving incomplete, and the entire picture has been altered. Indeed, it has been said that if one tiny chemical interaction out of a million had been different, the Universe as we know it would have been impossible.

If Barbara Marx Hubbard's life really *was* a "mystery story," and if we were "at the scene" with notebook in hand when she ended her life as a "regular human being" and began her life as a Universal Being, would we pick up the clues? Would we figure out how it happened?

Would we have seen, in advance, Barbara's decision to have lunch that November day all alone for the first time since coming to France, as *pivotal* in setting up the ideal circumstance for a "chance meeting" with the man she was going to marry?

Would we have seen, for that matter, her choice of France itself for her year of study abroad as crucial to the eventual playing out of her story? She could, after all, just as easily have chosen Sweet Briar's program for a year of study in Spain.

And what about Earl Hubbard arriving at Chez Rosalie at the precise moment when there was only one more seat left in the entire place?

Would it be clear to us at the outset, rather than obvious in retrospect, that Barbara's early life of privilege and her family's considerable wealth were *necessary* in order for the remaining dominoes to fall as they have?

Are we absolutely clear that were it not for this positioning, she could never have posed a question to the President of the United States that he could not answer—and that just *any* person not answering would never have ignited what a *President* failing to answer ignited within Barbara?

Is it as obvious to you as it is to me that all the frustrations of this woman's life led, step-by-step, to spiritual insights that could open the mind of humanity itself to ideas and ways of being that could end our *global* frustration?

This retro exploration could go on and on. But the point that I dearly hope you are getting here is that it is *not only Barbara's life* that has been uniquely and perfectly constructed to produce the Soul's desired outcomes—it is *all of ours.*

I am saying that every one of us, if we look at our lives in retrospect like this, will easily detect the clues that will unravel the mystery of our life in a way that will allow us to know at last Who We Really Are.

I am saying that Life has been *fixing it all along to tell us of that.*

When we see our past clearly like this, it is left only for us to bring that insight (the ability to *see in*) forward, looking ahead on this day with equal clarity about the perfection of all that is happening in this moment of our lives.

I urge you now to trust Life. Trust God. Trust the Universal Being that is *You.*

It is said that "necessity is the mother of invention." But that is wrong.

You are.

You are inventing your Self right now, at this moment, re-creating yourself anew in every nanosecond, in the next grandest version of the greatest vision you ever held about who you are. You are doing this either consciously or unconsciously, but you are doing it.

Go now, and experience your life as the wonder that it is. Participate actively, and with full awareness of what you are doing, in the process of evolution. Bring yourself today the experience for which your life was designed: *Conscious Evolution.*

Not out of *necessity,* but out of *desire.*

🌿 🌿 🌿

AFTERWORD

I believe that the thoughts of Barbara Marx Hubbard are among the most important articulations of spiritual and metaphysical truth brought to the human race in centuries. They bring us deep insight into our New Story.

In the following paragraphs, I have included some final excerpts from Barbara's journals to give you an insight into why Barbara, at 80, continues her work at an extraordinary pace and has chosen to make publications, documentary films, and DVDs continuously available to the public.

From the Journals of Barbara Marx Hubbard . . .

September 3, 2003
This morning, sitting up by the little cross at Mt. Calvary Monastery, I asked, "What shall I do with all this wonderful information coming through the Universal Self into my journal?"

> *YOU ARE TO REMEMBER IT at all times.*
> *Just as people read the Scripture every day, so are you to reread the Inner Scripture that is unfolding within you, and has been for many years.*

You can make a private book—almost a secret book—recording the mystery of what is happening within you to help you remember who you really are. It will only be available for those who ask for it. Do it for yourself and for any other selves drawn to it by word of mouth. It will eventually spread like wildfire; it is like the fire held in the arms of Homo erectus.

You are to do a small book. That is what you need to remember Me at all times, as your self-centered mind is being absorbed in your God-centered mind.

By doing so, you will remember every day. It is your daily word of your Universal Self, your Soul, now incarnating into your arising, yearning, earthly self. It is a form of "aural alchemy."

The key good news inherent in this view is that Universal Creativity, which has evolved a universe from subatomic particles to us, is the Force within us, pressuring us to evolve. We are not doing this alone.

Great Beings have come before us to pave The Way and open the doors to our next stage of evolution. Yet now, each of us can choose to enter this new space in consciousness ourselves—each of us can willingly intend to enter the Garden of Co-creation. Here we heal the wound of separation of the human and Divine within ourselves, and we begin the process of learning to join together to co-create new worlds. The Force is within us, pressing us, as we make the choice to consciously evolve.

For the first time on this earth, a species has gained the power to destroy its environment or evolve toward an unknown, universal future. Unconscious evolution has become conscious choice. We are The Generation With Choice. Our problems are evolutionary drivers to awaken our new potentials. The meaning of our new powers is to give us the capacity to restore the earth, free ourselves from hunger and poverty, liberate unique human creativity, shift from weaponry to "livingry" (as Buckminster Fuller put it), and begin the vast journey of the exploration of both inner and outer space.

I want to be a demonstration of *conscious* evolution, using my own presence and life story as a way to activate the evolutionary impulse in millions of people who are ready and longing for deeper life purpose and resonant community. I especially want to serve women who are shifting in their very nature from one biosocial role to the next. I can be a model for the emerging co-creative woman, an "elder from the future," to offer a hand to those who are now rising in leadership for our world.

I've been through the journey of the arising woman and am just now standing on tiptoe at the horizon of life, peering over to the Next Step, and looking backward to beckon others to come up higher and see their part in the new world that is being born in our midst.

(THE END OF EXCERPTS FROM BARBARA'S JOURNALS)

If you enjoyed the content you found in this book, you'll be happy to know that I spent three days in a television studio with Barbara in the winter of 2010 gathering background material for this book. For a wide-ranging exploration that brings Barbara into your life in a very personal way, you may wish to obtain the DVD set of those informal, delightful, and sometimes eyebrow-raising conversations. They may be ordered from either **www.evolve.org** or **www.nealedonaldwalsch.com**.

In addition, I recommend Barbara's award-winning documentary series *Humanity Ascending: A New Way Through Together*. In these transformational films, Barbara presents vital elements to awaken the codes for our own conscious evolution and offers direction, meaning, and a vision toward our birth as a new humanity. The address from which to obtain these films is the same: **www.evolve.org**. (Also available from this website is *The 52 Codes,* which was mentioned in Chapter 15.) An Additional Resources page for those wanting to follow up on the ideas and information presented in *The Mother of Invention* may be found on this site as well.

Finally, if you wish to join in co-creating the Day One event on December 22, 2012, you may do so also by going to **www .evolve.org**. I hope you will add your personal energies to Barbara's in collaborating on making this event a wonderful reality.

And if you would like to learn more about the Conversations with God Spiritual Mentoring Program that I have developed to help us all move through the 2012 transitional period, please visit **www.nealedonaldwalsch.com**. The three-month program includes 36 lessons on the most important messages in the CwG books, with personal one-on-one telephone coaching with me along the way.

Before we end here, I would like to thank and acknowledge some of the people who helped make this book possible—chief among them, Barbara Marx Hubbard herself, who gave me open access to all of her journals and notes from the past 50 years. Then, thanks to Bill Gladstone, literary agent extraordinaire and a wonderful author in his own right, who initially invited me to write this book. As well, to new friend Claudia Welss, who first suggested that I create the book as a work of *causal art;* and to Darrell Laham, to whom we owe the term "causal art" itself. Also, deep thanks to Lisa Mitchell, my editor at Hay House, who is the best editor I ever had. Wow. She actually makes me sound like a *good writer.* And finally to my wife, poet Em Claire, who managed, around her own considerably busy life, to nurse me through the long writing process with deep caring, wonderful knowing, and endless love.

Speaking for myself and my dear, dear friend Barbara, thank you all for taking this journey with us. We both sincerely hope that it has served you.

— **Neale Donald Walsch**
December 2010

ABOUT THE AUTHOR

With an early interest in religion and a deeply felt connection to spirituality, **Neale Donald Walsch** spent the majority of his life thriving professionally, yet searching for spiritual meaning before beginning his now-famous *Conversations with God* series. These books have been translated into 37 languages, touching millions and inspiring important changes in people's day-to-day lives. Seven of his 27 books have reached the *New York Times* best-sellers list.

Neale lives in Ashland, Oregon, with his wife, poet Em Claire. In 2001 he founded Humanity's Team, which he describes as a worldwide civil-rights movement for the soul (**www.Humanitys Team.org**). In 2005 he began work on putting into place a global education program, The School of the New Spirituality (**www .SchooloftheNewSpirituality.com**). In 2010 he created the CwG Spiritual Mentoring Program for individuals seeking to bring their highest spiritual understanding into their everyday lives.

Website: **www.NealeDonaldWalsch.com**

Hay House Titles of Related Interest

YOU CAN HEAL YOUR LIFE, *the movie,*
starring Louise L. Hay & Friends
(available as a 1-DVD program and an expanded 2-DVD set)
Watch the trailer at: **www.LouiseHayMovie.com**

THE SHIFT, *the movie,*
starring Dr. Wayne W. Dyer
(available as a 1-DVD program and an expanded 2-DVD set)
Watch the trailer at: **www.DyerMovie.com**

THE SECRET OF 2012 AND A NEW WORLD AGE, *Understanding*
Fractal Time
by Gregg Braden

INTRODUCING NEALE DONALD WALSCH:
God's Latest Scribe? from the producers of *Introducing Abraham:*
The Secret Behind THE SECRET (DVD)

MODERN-DAY MIRACLES: Miraculous Moments and Extraordinary
Stories from People All Over the World Whose Lives Have Been
Touched by Louise L. Hay, by Louise L. Hay & Friends

THE POWER OF INTENTION: Learning to Co-create
Your World Your Way, by Dr. Wayne W. Dyer

TRUTH, TRIUMPH, AND TRANSFORMATION: Sorting Out
the Fact from the Fiction in Universal Law, by Sandra Anne Taylor

WHAT DOES THAT MEAN? Exploring Mind, Meaning,
and Mysteries, by Eldon Taylor

All of the above are available at your local bookstore,
or may be ordered by contacting Hay House (see next page).

We hope you enjoyed this Hay House book.
If you would like to receive a free catalogue featuring additional
Hay House books and products, or if you would like information
about the Hay Foundation, please contact:

Hay House UK Ltd
292B Kensal Road • London W10 5BE
Tel: (44) 20 8962 1230; Fax: (44) 20 8962 1239
www.hayhouse.co.uk

***

Published and distributed in the United States of America by:
Hay House, Inc. • PO Box 5100 • Carlsbad, CA 92018-5100
Tel: (1) 760 431 7695 or (1) 800 654 5126;
Fax: (1) 760 431 6948 or (1) 800 650 5115
www.hayhouse.com

***

Published and distributed in Australia by:
Hay House Australia Ltd • 18/36 Ralph Street • Alexandria, NSW 2015
Tel: (61) 2 9669 4299, Fax: (61) 2 9669 4144
www.hayhouse.com.au

***

Published and distributed in the Republic of South Africa by:
Hay House SA (Pty) Ltd • PO Box 990 • Witkoppen 2068
Tel/Fax: (27) 11 467 8904
www.hayhouse.co.za

***

Published and distributed in India by:
Hay House Publishers India • Muskaan Complex • Plot No.3
B-2• Vasant Kunj • New Delhi - 110 070
Tel: (91) 11 41761620; Fax: (91) 11 41761630
www.hayhouse.co.in

***

Distributed in Canada by:
Raincoast • 9050 Shaughnessy St • Vancouver, BC V6P 6E5
Tel: (1) 604 323 7100
Fax: (1) 604 323 2600

***

Sign up via the Hay House UK website to receive the Hay House
online newsletter and stay informed about what's going on with your
favourite authors. You'll receive bimonthly announcements
about discounts and offers, special events, product highlights,
free excerpts, giveaways, and more!
www.hayhouse.co.uk

Heal Your Life One Thought at a Time . . . on Louise's All-New Website!

"Life is bringing me everything I need and more."

— Louise Hay

Come to HEALYOURLIFE.COM today and meet the world's best-selling self-help authors; the most popular leading intuitive, health, and success experts; up-and-coming inspirational writers; and new like-minded friends who will share their insights, experiences, personal stories, and wisdom so you can heal your life and the world around you . . . one thought at a time.

Here are just some of the things you'll get at HealYourLife.com:

- DAILY AFFIRMATIONS
- CAPTIVATING VIDEO CLIPS
- EXCLUSIVE BOOK REVIEWS
- AUTHOR BLOGS
- LIVE TWITTER AND FACEBOOK FEEDS
- BEHIND-THE-SCENES SCOOPS
- LIVE STREAMING RADIO
- "MY LIFE" COMMUNITY OF FRIENDS

PLUS:
FREE Monthly Contests and Polls
FREE BONUS gifts, discounts,
and newsletters

Make It Your Home Page Today!
www.HealYourLife.com®

HEAL YOUR LIFE®

JOIN THE HAY HOUSE FAMILY

As the leading self-help, mind, body and spirit publisher in the UK, we'd like to welcome you to our family so that you can enjoy all the benefits our website has to offer.

 **EXTRACTS** from a selection of your favourite author titles

 **COMPETITIONS, PRIZES & SPECIAL OFFERS** Win extracts, money off, downloads and so much more

 **LISTEN** to a range of radio interviews and our latest audio publications

 **CELEBRATE YOUR BIRTHDAY** An inspiring gift will be sent your way

 **LATEST NEWS** Keep up with the latest news from and about our authors

 **ATTEND OUR AUTHOR EVENTS** Be the first to hear about our author events

 **iPHONE APPS** Download your favourite app for your iPhone

 **HAY HOUSE INFORMATION** Ask us anything, all enquiries answered

join us online at **www.hayhouse.co.uk**

 292B Kensal Road, London W10 5BE
T: 020 8962 1230 E: info@hayhouse.co.uk